Y0-BEG-305

GREAT WORDS

Dr. Jack L. Arnold

CEP
Christian Education & Publications

A Leader's Guide for this book written by Dean Arnold and Carol
Arnold is available from the PCA Christian Education Bookstore.
Call 1.800.283.1357 or visit www.cepbookstore.com

CONTENTS

About the Author

Jack Arnold was the President and founder of Equipping Pastors International Inc, a missionary organization designed to train pastors anywhere in the world, with special emphasis on those who will never get an opportunity for a formal Biblical education.

Dr. Arnold served five very different pastorates over 37 years. He received his Master's and Doctor's degrees from Dallas Theological Seminary and was ordained in the Presbyterian Church in America. He was an adjunct professor at Reformed Theological Seminary Orlando and New Geneva Seminary and a visiting professor at Nairobi International School of Theology in Nairobi, Bible Institute of South Africa in Cape Town, Ukraine Biblical Seminary in Kiev, East Asia School of Theology in Singapore and Regent University School of Divinity. Dr. Arnold had a worldwide notes ministry, now available on www.thirdmill.org, which is being used in theological training by extension in many developing countries.

Jack died suddenly on January 9, 2005 while doing what he loved most—preaching. He was preaching to his former congregation and a large group of seminary students, telling them that God could call him home at any moment. Then he quoted his life verse, "For me to live is Christ;" and before he could finish the last part of the verse ("and to die is gain") the Lord did indeed call him home.

Jack leaves behind his wife, Carol, who resides in Orlando, Florida. They have 4 sons, all in various forms of ministry, and 14 grandchildren. Carol and son Dean have put together a Leader's Guide to go along with this book on the topic of Salvation.

chapter 1:

predestination

OBJECTIVES

- To know the biblical meaning of predestination.
- To be able to explain the different usages of predestination as found in the Bible.
- To understand the importance of the doctrine of predestination.
- To know the various aspects of God's predestinating work as it affects our relationship with God and other men.

"You are not one of those people who believes in predestination, are you?" This is a question that comes my way frequently, and it is said with such scorn that it makes me feel like believing in predestination is equivalent to having leprosy. It seems that no biblical doctrine is more likely to prove offensive to the unregenerate and spiritually immature than that of predestination.

Predestination is a biblical subject, and relates to our salvation in Christ. To deny election and predestination, one must tear out page after page of the Bible. However, it seems as though this doctrine is purposely avoided, even in many Bible-teaching pulpits, for fear of offending those in the pews. Predestination stirs people, and most pastors do not want the hassle of dealing with confused or angry saints or the embarrassment of losing potential members. Yet predestination is a biblical subject and it must not be avoided, for God has commanded ministers of the Gospel to preach the whole counsel of God. No pastor should be a manpleaser, and if the doctrine of predestination rubs some people the wrong way, so be it. Maybe they need to be challenged with God's sovereign purposes so as to cause them to bow humbly to the Sovereign God of the universe.

I have pleaded with some men to trust Christ, begged them to commit to Christ, and wept tears before them to put Christ as their Lord, but there is no response or interest. But let me preach on election and predestination and these same folks are stirred and ready to crucify me. Why? Because this doctrine really hits at the fact that man cannot save himself by his good works.

The subject of predestination is the meat of the Word, and it is for the more mature believers. There are many other doctrines we should learn and apply before we sink our teeth into the subjects of election and predestination. However, this does not mean we should never preach on the sovereign purposes of God. Just because this doctrine confuses some and offends others does not make it any less the Word of God. Nor should we stop preaching predestination because some have abused this doctrine by becoming fatalistic. The Apostle Paul was with the Thessalonians between two and six weeks. Yet, when he wrote them a few months later, he assumed and expected them to understand about election and predestination.

Spurgeon, as he sought to answer critics who said that the doctrine of election should not be preached because it has been so badly abused by some, said,

> That is popish doctrine! It was upon that very theory that priests kept back the Bible from the people. They did not give the Bible to them lest they should misuse it. "But," says the objector, "do not some men abuse the doctrines of grace?" I grant you that they do, but if we destroy everything that men abuse, we should have nothing left. What, are there to be no ropes because some fools hang themselves? And must knives be discarded as dangerous because some use them as weapons of destruction? Decidedly not! And. besides all this, remember that men do read the Scriptures and think about these doctrines, and therefore often make mistakes about them. Who shall set them right if we who preach the Word hold our tongues about the matter?

As Spurgeon said, we must set men right on their understanding of election and predestination, but this does not mean we should argue over the issue at the drop of a hat. Many who come to the truth of God's sovereign purposes in salvation go on personal crusades to convert every Christian to their newfound excitement. They often become more evangelistic for election and predestination than they are for Christ and His kingdom! We should have our convictions on the subject of election and predestination, and speak out on them when people are truly seeking some answers for life. But we should not spend five minutes arguing with people, for a man convinced against his will is of the same opinion still. You may convince a brother that predestination is true, but be so obnoxious in doing so that the brother is offended by your bad attitude. We are to hold the truth, but to speak it in love. Remember, God must reveal the truth of sovereign election and predestination to His people.

Martin Luther once said that folks who have lived long and suffered much are more ready to accept the teachings of election and predestination, for they desire answers to their sufferings and can find answers only in the sovereign purposes of God.

6

THE DEFINITION OF PREDESTINATION

The word "predestination" comes from the Greek *prooridzo*, which means "to mark out beforehand" or "to decide beforehand." The word *oridzo* means "to put a boundary around" or "to establish a limitation." The preposition *pro* means "before." Some have therefore defined "predestination" as "to fix" or "to appoint."

The word "predestination" as it relates to salvation refers only to God's elect. God marked out the elect and put a boundary around them and destined them to an ultimate end or purpose, which is salvation and conformity to Christ. When it is used of God's elect, predestination means a predetermining of the destiny of the elect. It looks to the ultimate end of God's choice, which is the saint's ultimate glorification.

In His purpose (plan), God foreknew, chose, appointed, and then predestined those He elected to be like Christ. God loved us and then chose us for salvation. He then appointed us (His elect) to eternal life and predestined us to be like Christ in heaven.

THE USAGE OF PREDESTINATION

PREDESTINATION OF CHRIST'S DEATH

> *For truly in this city there were gathered together against your holy servant Jesus, whom you anointed, both Herod and Pontius Pilate, along with the Gentiles and the peoples of Israel, to do whatever your hand and your plan had predestined to take place. (Acts 4:27-28)*

These verses tell us that Christ's death was no accident. It was part of God's sovereign purpose. He was predestined by God the Father to die. Everything about the death of Christ was planned, even the free actions of sinful men. God sent His Son, Jesus Christ, to accomplish our redemption through His death, while His murderers purposed otherwise. These verses tell us that predestination is equivalent to or a definite part of the plan of God.

> *This Jesus, delivered up according to the definite plan and foreknowledge of God, you crucified and killed by the hands of lawless men. (Acts 2:23)*

PREDESTINATED TO ADOPTION

> *In love he predestined us for adoption through Jesus Christ, according to the purpose of his will. (Eph. 1:4-5)*

This verse clearly teaches that the true Christian was predestined to be in God's family. God chose the Christian *"before the foundation of the world"* (Eph. 1:4). God then marked out the chosen ones to be adopted into God's family. God destined the elect to be adopted as sons through the death of Christ.

Notice carefully two aspects of God's predestination of His people. First, this act of predestination to salvation and adoption was done in love. The words "in love" in Eph. 1:4b should be read with Eph. 1:5: *"In love He predestined us."* Predestination is based on God's love, for all that we have as Christians comes through God's love and grace to us. To reject predestination is to reject a very important aspect of God's love to us. Second, this act of predestination was according to the "kind intention" or "good pleasure" of God's will. He marked us out to be His sons and daughters because He wanted to do it, not because He was compelled. God was under no obligation to save any of the sinful human race, but He did so because He loved us.

PREDESTINED TO A SPIRITUAL INHERITANCE

> *In him we have obtained an inheritance, having been predestined according to the purpose of him who works all things according to the counsel of his will. (Eph. 1:11)*

Our total inheritance in Christ is because God predestined us to it according to His purposes, after the counsel of His own will. We did not deserve salvation. We were not worthy of salvation. We were sinners going our own independent way and headed for eternal destruction, but God switched things around because He determined that we should be His children and be joint heirs with His Son, Jesus Christ. These truths are too wonderful for me!

PREDESTINED TO BE LIKE CHRIST

> *And we know that for those who love God all things work together for good, for those who are called according to his purpose. For those whom he foreknew he also predestined to be conformed to the image of his Son, in order that he might be the firstborn among many brothers. (Rom. 8:28-29)*

Those whom God loved (foreknew) according to His eternal purposes, He *"predestined to be conformed to the image of his Son."* The end, the goal, the design of predestination is to make the elected saint Christlike. God's ultimate purpose for the Christian is that he may share the spiritual image of Christ. Therefore, we can say that the ultimate purpose of predestinating the elect was that the image of God might be restored to a fallen race through the redeemed ones of the perfect plan.

God did not predestine His people only to heaven, but to Christlikeness. Christlikeness will be complete only when the elected saint is in heaven with his glorified body. However, we do not have to wait until we get to heaven to experience Christlikeness. Conformity to Christ is taking place now to some degree as the Holy Spirit works progressively in the life of the Christian who walks by faith.

> *And we all, with unveiled face, beholding the glory of the Lord, are being transformed into the same image from one degree of glory to another. For this comes from the Lord who is the Spirit. (2 Cor. 3:18)*

God's predestinating purpose can be compared to an artist who wants to sculpt the bust of a person from marble. The artist first conceives in his mind the image he wishes to make, and he never deviates from that plan. He chooses a block of rough marble and begins to chip away on that rough slab. At first it does not look like much, but the finished product is exactly what he predestined the image of the person to be. There was a great deal of chipping and smoothing off of the rough edges in order to get the final image. So it is with the Christian. We have been chosen by God and predestined to be conformed to His Son, Jesus Christ. God never gives up on His plan to make us Christlike. God chips away at our sin and smoothes off the rough edges of our lives. He never gives up on what He has conceived and planned for us to be. He wants us to have complete and perfect conformity to Christ in eternity.

THEOLOGICAL PROBLEMS

IS PREDESTINATION INCONSISTENT WITH 2 PETER 3:9?

If God has a plan that includes the salvation of the elect, how does this match up with the teaching that *"The Lord is not slow to fulfill his promise as some count slowness, but is patient toward you, not wishing that any should perish, but that all should reach repentance"* (2 Peter 3:9). This verse, and John 3:16, are probably the most used and abused verses in the Bible.

Universalism

If this verse is taken literally and one refers it to the sovereign will of God, then it teaches that all men will be saved ultimately. If God sovereignly wills that none shall perish, then none will perish and all will be saved. The Greek word for "willing" is *boulomai*, which in the Bible usually means "a planned purpose" or "a sovereign will." If this verse refers to salvation and the "any" and "all" refer to mankind in general, then this verse teaches universalism, that it is God's sovereign will that none should perish and all should come to repentance.

This interpretation contradicts the other teachings of Scripture, for we know that not all men will be saved.

Whoever believes in the Son has eternal life; whoever does not obey the Son shall not see life, but the wrath of God remains on him. (John 3:36)

Desire of God

Most Bible scholars make a distinction between the desire and the sovereign will of God—that it is not God's emotional desire that any should perish, but in the hidden plan some do perish.

Three aspects of the will of God may be observed in scripture: (1) the sovereign will of God; (2) the moral will of God, and (3) the desire of God coming from His heart of love. The sovereign will of God is certain of complete fulfillment, but the moral law is disobeyed by men, and the desires of God are fulfilled only to the extent that they are included in His sovereign will. God does not desire that any should perish, but it is clear that many will not be saved. *(Scofield Bible)*

This view has several weaknesses that the keen Bible student must face. First, the word for "willing" is *boulomai*, which usually means "a planned purpose," referring to God's sovereign will. It is difficult to translate this as "desire" or "wish." Second, it is difficult to make a distinction between God's will and God's desires, for the Bible seems to indicate that all of God's desires do come to pass.

But he is unchangeable, and who can turn him back? What he desires, that he does. (Job 23:13)

Elect of God

I believe the above explanations are not satisfying to the insightful Bible student, so he must search deeper for the meaning of this verse. The context of 2 Peter 3 must be taken into consideration. The context is about false teachers who were denying the promise of Christ's second coming. *"Knowing this first of all, that scoffers will come in the last days with scoffing, following their own sinful desires. They will say, 'Where is the promise of his coming? For ever since the fathers fell asleep, all things are continuing as they were from the beginning of creation'"* (2 Pet. 3:3-4). Peter assures the Christian that the Lord will return in His own time. *"But do not overlook this one fact, beloved, that with the Lord one day is as a thousand years, and a thousand years as one day"* (2 Pet. 3:8). Notice carefully that he is talking to the "beloved." God is not slow concerning the promise of the return of His Son and is patient toward true Christians, His people. *"The Lord is not slow to fulfill his promise as some count slowness, but is patient toward you, not wishing that any should*

10

perish, but that all should reach repentance" (2 Pet. 3:9). Notice God is patient toward "you," and this refers back to the "beloved" who are Christians. Who do the "any" and "all" refer to in context? What is the nearest antecedent to "any?" It is the "you" that refers back to the "beloved," who are Christians. "Any" and "all," therefore, refer to the total community of God's elect whom He will save before the second advent of Christ.

It is God's sovereign will or determined purpose to save all the elect of the church before the Lord Jesus returns. This explanation fits the context grammatically, contextually, and theologically. In light of this interpretation, there is no inconsistency between God's sovereign election and 2 Pet. 3:9.

IS PREDESTINATION INCONSISTENT WITH 1 TIMOTHY 2:4?

> *This is good, and it is pleasing in the sight of God our Savior, who desires all people to be saved and to come to the knowledge of the truth. (1 Tim. 2:3-4)*

Desire of God

This passage may refer to the emotional will of God and not His sovereign will, because it uses the Greek word *thelo,* which often means "wish" or "desire." Therefore, it is God's emotional will (desire) to save all men, but in His secret plan it is not His sovereign will to save all men.

All Who Come to the Truth

The word *thelo* does sometimes refer to God's sovereign will. *"But to all who did receive him, who believed in his name, he gave the right to become children of God, who were born, not of blood nor of the will of the flesh nor of the will of man, but of God"* (John 1:12-13) and *"So then he has mercy on whomever he wills, and he hardens whomever he wills"* (Rom. 9:18). Furthermore, the Bible speaks of God bringing all of His desires to pass. *"But he is unchangeable, and who can turn him back? What he desires, that he does"* (Job 23:13). The "all" in 1 Tim. 2:4 must be given a limited meaning and refer to all who believe ("come to the knowledge of the truth"), and these are the elect of God.

Conclusion

It is better to take 1 Timothy 2:4 as the emotional will, wish, or desire of God, even though it is difficult for us to understand how God could have desires apart from His secret plan. This is just another mystery we cannot grasp because we are finite. That God desires to save all men seems to be consistent with Ezekiel 33:11 in which God declares, *"Say to them, As I live, declares the Lord GOD, I have no pleasure in the death of the wicked, but that the wicked turn from his way and live; turn back, turn back from your evil ways, for why will you die, O house of Israel?"* God takes no pleasure in seeing the wicked lost, but He must do so in order to guard His own justice, His own character.

IS PREDESTINATION A HINDRANCE TO PRAYER?

Absolutely not! Because God has a plan, we know He has the power and wisdom to answer our prayers. Whenever we ask anything in God's will we receive answers to prayer. *"And this is the confidence that we have toward him, that if we ask anything according to his will he hears us"* (1 John 5:14). God says we have not, because we ask not. We must come to God with all our requests, believing in simple faith. We must let God determine whether our prayers are in His will.

We must remember that God's plan includes prayer as a means of bringing about His plan to save men. *"Brothers, my heart's desire and prayer to God for them is that they may be saved"* (Rom. 10:1). God desires for His people to be colaborers with Him in the salvation of souls, and prayer allows us to see God work His plan through us. We must pray always. *"And he told them a parable to the effect that they ought always to pray and not lose heart"* (Luke 18:1). When we pray, we see God work supernaturally. When we do not pray, God does not work supernaturally in our experience. A person who says he or she believes in the sovereign purposes of God in salvation and is not a person of prayer is a hypocrite.

Perhaps if Christians would spend more time in prayer pleading with God for the souls of men and less time superficially begging men to come to Christ, we would have more experience of seeing people genuinely saved.

We pray for the salvation of the lost because we know that God must move upon the lost before they will respond to Christ. We pray because we know that God has the power to change their stubborn wills. God must work supernaturally upon a sinner before the person can trust in Christ, and God has ordained that our prayers should be used to bring about the salvation of men.

A pastor told me of his rebellious fifteen-year-old son who wanted nothing to do with Christianity. The pastor said, "Jack, if I did not believe in God's ability to overrule in my son's life, I would lose my mind. If I thought my son had total free will, then I would never have any hope that he would be saved, for his natural will does not want to turn to God. My confidence is in God, not in my son. God must intervene!

HOW TO KNOW ONE IS ELECTED AND PREDESTINED TO SALVATION?

People often get shaky when they hear about predestination and wonder whether they are truly among the elect of God. The Bible gives some evidences that a person may test to see whether he is among the elect.

The Elect Respond to the Gospel

For we know, brothers loved by God, that he has chosen you, because our gospel came to you not only in word, but also in power and in the Holy Spirit and with full conviction. You know what kind of men we proved to be among you for your sake. And you became imitators of us and of the Lord, for you received the word in much affliction, with the joy of the Holy Spirit. (1 Thess. 1:46)

When a sinner responds to the terms of the Gospel and receives Christ by faith, then he knows he is numbered among the elect.

The Elect Manifest Obedience to Christ

To those who are elect exiles ... according to the foreknowledge of God the Father, in the sanctification of the Spirit, for obedience to Jesus Christ and for sprinkling with his blood. (1 Pet. 1:12)

This obedience is the initial command to trust Christ and demonstrate a desire to be obedient to Christ as a Christian.

The Elect Manifest Faith, Love and Steadfastness

Remembering before our God and Father your work of faith and labor of love and steadfastness of hope in our Lord Jesus Christ. For we know, brothers loved by God, that he has chosen you. (1 Thess. 1:3-4)

These virtues will show up to some degree in the true child of God.

The Elect Follow Christ

"But you do not believe because you are not part of my flock. My sheep hear my voice, and I know them, and they follow me." (John 10:26-27)

Jesus told the unbelieving Jews that they did not believe because they were not of His sheep (elect), but that His sheep hear His voice and follow Him. They follow Christ, not men, not organizations, not systems, but Christ!

The Elect Make Their Election Sure by Doing Good Works

Therefore, brothers, be all the more diligent to make your calling and election sure, for if you practice these qualities you will never fall. (2 Pet. 1:10)

God's elect have a desire to please Christ with their life.

> *For this very reason, make every effort to supplement your faith with virtue, and virtue with knowledge, and knowledge with self-control, and self-control with steadfastness, and steadfastness with godliness, and godliness with brotherly affection, and brotherly affection with love. For if these qualities are yours and are increasing, they keep you from being ineffective or unfruitful in the knowledge of our Lord Jesus Christ.   (2 Pet. 1:58)*

Good works never save a person. Only Christ can save through faith in Him. However, good works give us the evidence or demonstrate the reality of our election in Christ. Christians make their election sure in their experience by good works.

> *Put on then, as God's chosen ones, holy and beloved, compassion, kindness, humility, meekness, and patience, bearing with one another and, if one has a complaint against another, forgiving each other; as the Lord has forgiven you, so you also must forgive. (Col. 3:12-13)*

THE ELECT PERSEVERE TO THE END

> *And we know that for those who love God all things work together for good, for those who are called according to his purpose. For those whom he foreknew he also predestined to be conformed to the image of his Son, in order that he might be the firstborn among many brothers. And those whom he predestined he also called, and those whom he called he also justified, and those whom he justified he also glorified. (Rom. 3:28-30)*

We can rest assured that every person whom God foreknew, predestined, called, justified, and glorified will make it to heaven. These also will persevere on earth.

This does not mean that a Christian cannot slip out of fellowship with Christ, or that an elect person lives a perfect life. The elect of God sometimes rebel, but when they do, God brings deep conviction to their souls about their sin. The elect child of God will have his ups and downs spiritually, but he will persevere to the end.

QUESTIONS:
1. From what you have learned from this chapter and from your study of the Bible, how would you define the word "predestination"?
2. What are the different usages of "predestination" in the Bible?
3. Explain the importance of a biblical view of predestination for our understanding of the relationship of God and man.
4. Prepare an outline of what you would say to defend the doctrine of predestination, and look for an opportunity to share it this week.

chapter 2:
salvation

OBJECTIVES

- To know how the Bible defines the word "salvation."
- To know the means that God uses to bring about salvation.
- To understand the past, present, and future nature of salvation and how it works throughout a person's life.
- To be able to explain the time aspects of salvation, and how God can be the first cause in a human decision for Christ.

What does it mean to be saved? The doctrine of salvation is a basic biblical truth and teaching, and yet there is probably no concept more misused and abused in nonChristian and even some Christian circles. Often we will hear a Christian give his testimony and say, "I have been gloriously saved by Christ. He has taken all my sins away." Yet those who know this person realize that he is still very much a sinner and quite vulnerable to sin. Furthermore, how many of us have sung the rousing chorus, "Gone, gone, gone, gone, yes, my sins are gone! Now I'm free and in my heart's a song"? What do we mean when we say we have been saved and our sins are gone?

As Christians, we know from our experience that we are saved because Christ has done a great work for us and has invaded our lives, but do we understand doctrinally what has happened to us, and can we explain it in a simple way to others? We must never veer from the simplicity of the Gospel.

THE DEFINITION AND CONCEPT OF SALVATION

The word "salvation" means "to deliver" or "to make safe." Therefore, salvation means that God delivers men from something and makes them safe in something.

The Bible declares dogmatically that salvation resides only in the person of Jesus Christ. *"And there is salvation in no one else [but Jesus], for there is no other name under heaven given among men by which we must be saved"* (Acts 4:12). *"Jesus* said to him, '*I am the way, and the truth, and the life. No one comes to the Father except through me*'" (John 14:6). If men are ever to be delivered and become safe, it can be only by, in, and through the person of Jesus Christ.

The Bible declares that salvation is always from sin. *"The saying is trustworthy and deserving of full acceptance, that Christ Jesus came into the world to save sinners, of whom I am the foremost"* (1 Tim. 1:15). Christ also came into this world to deliver His people from their sins. *"'She will bear a son, and you shall call his name Jesus, for he will save his people from their sins'"* (Matt. 1:21). What is sin? Sin is lawlessness. Sin is rebellion against God's moral law. Sin is acting independently of God.

Sin includes not only the more gross and obvious sins such as drunkenness, drug addiction, premarital sex, extramarital sex, homosexuality, stealing, and so on, but also the more subtle sins such as greed, hate, envy, jealousy, gossip, pride, and so forth. Sin separates men spiritually from God so that sinners are spiritually dead. *"For the wages of sin is death, but the free gift of God is eternal life in Christ Jesus our Lord"* (Rom. 6:23). Sin is what stirs God's holy wrath and causes Him to exercise justice and cast men into hell.

Men need a Savior. The word "Savior" means a deliverer. From what does the Bible say we need to be delivered? The world needs a Savior to deliver people from sin and the consequences of sin, which is eternal punishment. *"Since, therefore, we have now been justified by his blood, much more shall we be saved by him from the wrath of God"* (Rom. 5:9). The great need of the world is for a sin-bearer, not a joy-giver. We hear much about the need of men coming to Christ so He can give them joy, peace, and happiness. Christ is presented as the great joy-giver who helps men in their psychological problems. Christ is often preached as the Great Psychiatrist instead of the Great Physician who heals from sin. Do not misunderstand me: Christ *does* bring joy, peace, and happiness to sinners who come to Him. However, men lack joy, peace, and happiness because they are sinners and need to be saved from their sin. Many people call to Christ for some kind of psychological joy, peace, and happiness, and never understand that they are sinners in great need of Christ's cleansing. People cannot be saved until they realize they are sinful and come to Christ as poor, humble sinners who need forgiveness and a new life from God.

The Bible also clearly teaches that salvation involves making a sinner who has fled to Christ safe from sin, Satan, and hell. God declares that sin shall not rule over a true Christian. *"For sin will have no dominion over you, since you are not under law but under grace"* (Rom. 6:14). He has removed the believer positionally out of Satan's kingdom and into Christ's kingdom. *"He has delivered us from the domain of darkness and transferred us to the kingdom of his beloved Son"* (Col. 1:13). Furthermore, God has made the Christian free from His wrath. *"There is therefore now no condemnation for those who are in Christ Jesus"* (Rom. 8:1).

THE MEANS OF SALVATION

If it is true that salvation from sin, Satan, and hell resides solely in Jesus Christ, then the next logical question is: how can a person become saved? The Scriptures declare over and over again that salvation is through faith in Jesus Christ. *"For by grace you have been saved through faith. And this is not your own doing; it is the gift of God, not a result of works, so that no one may boast"* (Eph. 2:8-9). The Philippian jailer once asked the Apostle Paul and Silas, *"'Sirs, what must I do to be saved?'"* (Acts 16:30). They answered, *"'Believe in the Lord Jesus, and you will be saved, you and your household'"* (Acts 16:31). Faith in Christ is accepting the fact that He died for our sins and entrusting ourselves to His care and keeping.

Salvation is appropriated through faith in Jesus Christ. Notice that the object of faith is Christ, not Buddha, not Confucius, not Mohammed, not Moses, not any man or religious system. Only Christ. Salvation involves a personal commitment to Jesus Christ.

Again, I want to stress the importance of one's motive for trusting in Christ. Salvation comes only when someone sees himself a sinner in desperate need of cleansing. Often I hear preachers and evangelists say that if people will come to Christ, He will take away all their ills and pills. If they will trust Christ, He will solve all their problems. If they will believe in Christ, they will become more successful in business or on the athletic field or elsewhere. It may be true that if a person becomes a Christian, he will feel better physically (physical health is related to mental health and mental health to the freedom from guilt), and he will probably be able to cope better with problems, and he may even become a better businessman and athlete, but these are all byproducts of coming to Christ as a needy sinner.

Even Christians get sick and die. They have problems and they do not always succeed, but they always have a God who loves them, who has cleansed them, and who has promised them heaven's glory.

Only Christians can sing this song and mean it:

> *Dear dying Lamb, Thy precious blood*
> *Shall never lose its pow'r,*
> *'Til all the ransomed church of God*
> *Be saved and sin no more.*
> *(William Cowper, "There Is a Fountain")*

The Three Phases of Salvation

When people talk about salvation, they usually talk in terms of when they first trusted Christ as Lord and Savior. Many Christians never advance much beyond that initial salvation experience because they do not know that trusting Christ merely begins a process that will culminate in heaven. Initial salvation is the beginning, not the end. Salvation encompasses the whole of one's life and all of eternity, because salvation is past, present, and future.

Recently, I heard of a young man who made a profession of faith in Christ. His decision was made on a minimum of knowledge. He went to another Christian to share his decision for Christ. The older, more mature Christian said, "Howard, where do you go from here?" And the young man answered, "What else is there?"

Past Salvation

Salvation for us had a beginning. It began the moment we trusted in Christ as personal Lord and Savior: *"By grace you have been saved"* (Eph. 2:5). *"For by grace you have been saved through faith"* (Eph. 2:8). *"Believe in the Lord Jesus Christ, and you shall be saved ..."* (Acts 16:31). At a point in time, God delivered us judicially or positionally from our sins. We were still sinners, but God declared our sins were gone as far as He was concerned because Christ bore our sins. God put our sins on Christ. In a moment, Christ put our sins behind Him, removed them as far as the east is from the west, and put them at the bottom of the deepest sea.

When speaking of past salvation, we say theologically that Christ delivered us from the guilt and the penalty of sin. We stood condemned by a holy God, and His wrath burned hot against us. We were under God's judicial penalty, but Christ bore the penalty for us, and we were delivered. We were also guilty before God. We were burdened, distraught, and frustrated with the guilt of sin, but Christ cleansed us and lifted that burden, setting us free in Christ.

Do you remember when you were first saved and how you could breathe a sigh of relief because the guilt of your secret life of sin was forgiven by Christ? It was just as though a heavy weight was lifted off your soul. Your sins were gone, and you now can legitimately sing, "Gone, gone, gone, gone; yes, my sins are gone. Now I'm free and in my heart's a song." Your sins are gone judicially and positionally in Christ. The theological term given to this past salvation is *justification*.

Present Salvation

Salvation for us came the moment we bent our rebellious wills to the sovereign Christ, yet that was just the beginning. At the point of initial salvation, God began in us a process. *"For we are the aroma of Christ to God among those who are being saved and among those who are perishing"* (2 Cor. 2:15). Notice that we not only *have been* saved, but we *are being* saved. God is working in our experience. *"Therefore, my beloved, as you have always obeyed, so now, not only as in my presence but much more in my absence, work out your own salvation with fear and trembling, for it is God who works in you, both to will and to work for his good pleasure"* (Phil. 2:12-13). Daily, through every experience of life, God is saving us. God is delivering us from the power of sin in our experience. As Christians, we still have a sin nature — even though it has been positionally judged in Christ — and we need deliverance from sins in our daily life. We need a Savior every day because sin is such a powerful force in us. Each day we are being changed to conform more and more to the person of Jesus Christ. *"And we all, with unveiled face, beholding the glory of the Lord, are being transformed into the same image from one degree of glory to another. For this comes from the Lord who is the Spirit"* (2 Cor. 3:18). This is an experiential, continual, and progressive process until we die or until Christ comes for us at His second coming. The theological term given to this present salvation is *progressive sanctification*.

Christians can now claim with great confidence:

I would not work, my soul to save
For that my Lord has done;
But I would work like any slave
For love of God's dear Son.

FUTURE SALVATION

Salvation is also ultimate and final. Salvation that is begun and continued will be culminated when the Christian in eternity receives his new, redeemed body. *"Who [Christians] by God's power are being guarded through faith for a salvation ready to be revealed in the last time"* (1 Pet. 1:5). *"And not only the creation, but we ourselves, who have the firstfruits of the Spirit, groan inwardly as we wait eagerly for adoption as sons, the redemption of our bodies"* (Rom. 8:23). The Christian then will be delivered from the presence of sin. He will become what God initially saved him to be. The Christian will be perfect—no more pain, suffering, lust, conflict with sin, tears. Oh, what glory that will be! The theological term for this future salvation is *glorification*.

SUMMARY

Now if anyone asks you whether you are saved, you should answer, "Yes, *I have been saved* positionally from the penalty and guilt of sin; *I am being saved* from the power of sin in my experience; and *I shall be saved* from the presence of sin in heaven." We tend to think of our salvation as a point in time past, yet it is more accurate to think of it as a line that begins at conversion and ends in eternity future.

THE WONDERS OF SALVATION

Salvation is so simple that the smallest child can grasp it, and yet so profound that the greatest minds and the sharpest intellects cannot comprehend it fully. It is impossible to exhaust the depths of salvation because we are finite men trying to grasp the mind of an infinite God.

If we have been in Sunday School or around much good doctrinal teaching, we have probably heard that God the Father purposed and planned our salvation, God the Son procured and secured our salvation, and God the Holy Spirit applied our salvation. But what does all this mean? I will now speak of things that will boggle your mind and make it go "tilt." The question is, "When were you saved?"

SAVED IN THE ETEERNAL COUNCILS

Since God planned and purposed our salvation, He loved us in the eternal councils and knew that we would be saved. *"Even as he chose us in him before the foundation of the world, that we should be holy and blameless before him ..."* (Eph. 1:4). *"But we ought always to give thanks to God for you, brothers beloved by the Lord, because God chose you as the firstfruits to be saved, through sanctification by the Spirit and belief in the truth"* (2 Thess. 2:13). There is a sense in which we were saved conceptually in the mind of God before the world began, for there is no past, present, or future for God.

SAVED AT THE CROSS

Since Jesus Christ procured and secured our salvation, we must have been in Christ when He died for sinners: the Bible says, *"For I delivered to you as of first importance what I also received: that Christ died for our sins in accordance with the Scriptures"* (1 Cor. 15:3). Before we ever existed, Christ died in our place as a sinner's substitute. *"For our sake he made him to be sin who knew no sin, so that in him we might become the righteousness of God"* (2 Cor. 5:21). When Christ cried out from the cross, *"It is finished!"* (John 19:30), He made a complete and perfect sacrifice for our sins. At that moment, Christ died for every sin the Christian would ever commit—past, present, and future. *"Consequently, he is able to save to the uttermost those who draw near to God through him, since he always lives to make intercession for them"* (Heb. 7:25). He died for us, knowing all about our godless and sinful lives before conversion to Christ. He died for us, knowing of all the sins we would do after conversion and how many times we would fail Him. Oh, what love! Oh, what grace! Oh, what mercy! Christ positionally saved us at the cross.

SAVED AT THE APPOINTED TIME

Since the Holy Spirit applied our salvation, we know it was sovereign love and grace that caused the Holy Spirit to convict, draw, and regenerate us, enabling us to receive the Lord Jesus Christ when we were yet deep in our sins. *"And when the Gentiles heard this, they began rejoicing and glorifying the word of the Lord, and as many as were appointed to eternal life believed"* (Acts 13:48). *"And when he comes, he will convict the world concerning sin and righteousness and judgment"* (John 16:8). *"Jesus answered, 'Truly, truly, I say to you, unless one is born of water and the Spirit, he cannot enter the kingdom of God'"* (John 3:5). The Holy Spirit actually saved us at the appointed time.

SAVED EXPERIENTIALLY IN TIME TIME

Even though salvation is a total work of the Trinity, this does not eliminate the necessity for a person to exercise faith in the Lord Jesus Christ. No one will be saved in his experience until he trusts in Jesus Christ by an act of his own will. *"Because, if you confess with your mouth that Jesus is Lord and believe in your heart that God raised him from the dead, you will be saved. For with the heart one believes and is justified, and with the mouth one confesses and is saved"* (Rom. 10:9-10). *"For 'everyone who calls on the name of the Lord will be saved'"* (Rom. 10:13).

SUMMARY

We may never understand salvation completely as it relates to the eternal plans and purposes of God, but we can understand that it is faith in Christ that brings salvation. Lay hold of this truth. Burn this truth deep in your mind. It is faith in Christ plus nothing else that saves a sinner, and behind that faith is God's grace.

We experience the same bafflement that the hymn writer expressed in "I Know Whom I Have Believed." He knew God had worked grace in his heart, but intellectually he had a hard time understanding it. He said,

I know not how this saving faith
To me He did impart,
Nor how believing in His Word
Wrought peace within my heart.

I know not how the Spirit moves,
Convincing us of sin,
Revealing Jesus through the Word,
Creating faith in Him.

But I know Whom I have believed
And am persuaded that He is able
To keep that which I've committed
Unto Him against that day.

(Daniel M. Whittle, "I know Whom I Have believed")

THE CAUSE OF SALVATION

The Bible clearly states that God is the cause of our salvation. Jonah in the Old Testament made a prophetic utterance when he said, *"Salvation belongs to the LORD!"* (Jonah 2:9). The New Testament teaches that God is the first cause in our salvation. *"And I am sure of this, that he who began a good work in you will bring it to completion at the day of Jesus Christ"* (Phil. 1:6). *"Who saved us and called us to a holy calling, not because of our works but because of his own purpose and grace, which he gave us in Christ Jesus before the ages began"* (2 Tim. 1:9). It is God's pure, free grace that has caused our salvation to come to pass. *"For by grace you have been saved through faith. And this is not your own doing; it is the gift of God"* (Eph. 2:8). God alone gets all the glory for our salvation. *"For from him and through him and to him are all things. To him be glory forever. Amen"* (Rom. 11:36).

EXPERIENCE

We as Christians may have a difficult time understanding how God is the first cause in our salvation, while we know we had to make a decision for Christ in order to be saved. Admittedly, this is one of the great mysteries of the Bible. Some Christians never seem to intellectually accept the fact that God is the author of their salvation. They stumble over the doctrine and theology of God's sovereign purposes and often miss the blessing of grasping something of God's full and free grace. These dear ones will never appreciate their salvation as much as they could if they understood sovereign grace. In their experience, however, I believe all Christians know that God is the author and finisher of salvation. All Christians have a practice better than their theology and a heart for God better than a head of doctrine. God is the author and finisher of their faith whether they understand it intellectually or not.

First, every Christian thanks God for his salvation. The Christian gives thanks because he knows deep in his heart that God is responsible for his salvation. He knows that his salvation was not by chance or accident. Experience tells him that God worked in him before he came to Christ. After he comes to Christ, he gives God thanks for working grace in his heart.

Second, all Christians know God is the author of salvation because they pray for the conversion of others. Men do not pray for God to bring lost men partway to salvation so men can come the rest of the way. Instead, all Christians pray, "God save sinners!" They know experientially that God must open their eyes of understanding, soften their hard hearts, and turn their stubborn wills if they are to be saved. On our knees, all Christians believe in God's sovereign purposes to save men. The problem is that when we get up and write what we prayed, some of us become confused about allowing a sovereign God to do what He pleases.

J. I. Packer, in his excellent book, *Evangelism and the Sovereignty of God*, makes a profound statement:

> The situation is not what it seems to be. For it is not true that some Christians believe in divine sovereignty while others hold an opposite view. What is true is that all Christians believe in divine sovereignty, but some are not aware that they do, and mistakenly imagine and insist that they reject it. What causes this odd state of affairs? The root cause is the same as in most cases of error in the Church the intruding of rationalistic speculations, the passion for systematic consistency, a reluctance to recognize the existence of mystery and to let God be wiser than men, and a consequent subjecting of Scripture to the supposed demands of logic.

CONCLUSION

The greatest question that can be asked is, "What must I do to be saved?" And God's answer is, *"Believe in the Lord Jesus, and you will be saved"* (Acts 16:31). "How do I know that a sovereign God will save me if I do come to Christ?" *"[He] desires all people to be saved and to come to the knowledge of the truth"* (1 Tim. 2:4). Furthermore, Christ said He is anxious for men to respond to Him. *"For the Son of Man came to seek and to save the lost"* (Luke 19:10). God has promised to save all who come to Christ in simple faith. *"Whoever believes in the Son has eternal life; whoever does not obey the Son shall not see life, but the wrath of God remains on him"* (John 3:36). God cannot lie, and God cannot go back on His Word. God will not turn away one sinner who genuinely comes to Jesus Christ for salvation, for God is faithful.

Christ saves sinners. This is the Gospel message. He died for His church, taking her sins on Himself. When we trust in Jesus as our Lord and Savior we are declared righteous in the sight of God, but our salvation does not stop there. The believer continues to grow in Christ-likeness for the rest of his life, conforming Himself to the image of our Lord until he is with Him in eternity.

QUESTIONS:

1. From what you have learned from this chapter and from your study of the Bible, how would you define the word "salvation"?
2. Explain the importance of faith in a person's salvation.
3. How does your past experience of salvation affect how you live today?
4. How would you explain to someone else what he or she must do to be saved?

chapter 3:

gospel

OBJECTIVES

- To know what the Bible means by the word "gospel."
- To recognize when "gospel" is being applied to something that falls short of the biblical picture.
- To grasp and believe that the Bible is God-centered and not man-centered.
- To be able to explain the gospel message to someone else.

Do you believe and declare the true Gospel? I ask this because, in the twenty-first century, there is much preaching about the Gospel that may not be the biblical Gospel at all. This generation may well experience a scarcity of the true, biblical Gospel. The church is faced with what may be its greatest challenge. This challenge is not one of proclaiming the Gospel, for Christians have been doing that for two thousand years, but one of preserving the Gospel. The Gospel today is in danger of losing its meaning, even to many who profess to be Christians. The tragedy is that many false, perverted, and defective "gospels" are being preached, and many evangelicals do not have the discernment to know what is happening.

The Gospel is central to Christianity, and without a right preaching of the Gospel there is no Christianity. The Gospel is God's power for salvation of a human soul. *"For I am not ashamed of the gospel, for it is the power of God for salvation to everyone who believes, to the Jew first and also to the Greek"* (Rom. 1:16). Because it is God's power for salvation, the Gospel is to be preached to every creature. *"And [Jesus] said to them, 'Go into all the world and proclaim the gospel to the whole creation'"* (Mark 16:15). It is therefore absolutely essential that the Gospel be kept pure from error and protected from compromise. Just as the apostles were entrusted by God with the Gospel and were held responsible to proclaim it, so are we in the twenty-first century. *"But just as we have been approved by God to be entrusted with the gospel, so we speak, not to please man, but to please God who tests our hearts"* (1 Thess. 2:4). So burdened was the Apostle Paul to faithfully declare the Gospel, he said, *"For if I preach the gospel, that gives me no ground for boasting. For necessity is laid upon me. Woe to me if I do not preach the gospel!"* (1 Cor.

9:16). All efforts and all precautions must be taken to preserve the biblical Gospel. There is only one Gospel and that is the biblical Gospel, and anyone who does not preach this true Gospel is accursed.

> *I am astonished that you are so quickly deserting him who called you in the grace of Christ and are turning to a different gospel— not that there is another one, but there are some who trouble you and want to distort the gospel of Christ. But even if we or an angel from heaven should preach to you a gospel contrary to the one we preached to you, let him be accursed. (Gal. 1:6-8)*

The right preaching of the Gospel is essential, for there is only one Gospel that can save, and to believe any other Gospel is to be lost no matter how sincere one might be. To preach or believe a different Gospel brings a curse—but what about a defective Gospel? Our problem today among evangelicals is not the preaching of a wholly other Gospel but of a defective Gospel. Obviously, the Gospel that is being preached in many circles today is not a full or complete Gospel, but there is enough truth in it that one can be saved. God is gracious and saves people who respond to the simple Gospel. "Christ died for sinners and all who receive Him shall be saved." The basic problem is that a simple Gospel, not surrounded in good doctrinal content, often becomes a defective Gospel, and a defective Gospel often becomes a perverted Gospel. Many evangelicals today are caught up in a defective Gospel which in a few years will result in a perverted Gospel. What Gospel will the next generation believe?

Unannounced and undetected by most, there has come in modern times this new Gospel in evangelical circles. The new Gospel is in some ways like the biblical Gospel but it is very different in other ways. The likenesses are superficial but the differences are fundamental.

There is no doubt that Evangelicalism today is in a state of perplexity and unsettlement. In such matters as the practice of evangelism, the teaching of holiness, the building up of local church life, the pastor's dealing with souls, and the exercise of discipline, there is widespread dissatisfaction with things as they are and equally widespread uncertainty as to the road ahead. This is a complex phenomenon, to which many factors have contributed; but, if we go to the root of the matter, we shall find that these perplexities are all ultimately due to our having lost our grip on the biblical Gospel. Without realizing it, we have during the past century bartered the Gospel for a substitute product which, though it looks similar in points of detail, is as a whole a decidedly different thing. The new Gospel consequently fails to produce deep reverence, deep repentance, deep humility, a spirit of worship, a concern for the church. Why? We would suggest that the reason lies in its own character and content. It fails to make men Godcentered in their thoughts and Godfearing in their hearts because this is not primarily what it is trying to do. (J. I. Packer, Introductory Essay to John Owen's *The Death of Death in the Death of Christ*)

As we approach the subject of the biblical Gospel versus the new Gospel, I have no desire to flay my evangelical brethren personally, for I love them, but there is a need to expose the subtle attacks of the devil on the true Gospel. I hope that evangelicals will read this and return to a biblical emphasis in the content and preaching of the Gospel. My purpose in this chapter is to point out that the new Gospel has been derived from a weak or wrong theology.

From the new Cross has sprung a new philosophy of the Christian life, and from that new philosophy has come a new evangelical technique — a new type of meeting and a new kind of preaching. This new evangelism employs the same language as the old, but its content is not the same and its emphasis not as before. (A. W. Tozer, *The Old Cross and the New*)

THE BIBLICAL GOSPEL

The word "gospel" means "good news." The Gospel of Jesus Christ has tremendous news in it, for it tells a person how to be delivered from the guilt and penalty of sin, and how to escape the consequences of that sin — eternal judgment. The Gospel tells men how they can find peace with God and enjoy Him forever. The Gospel is good news because in it a person can understand that God has a purpose for his life and that in Christ there is abundant life. *"The thief comes only to steal and kill and destroy. I came that they may have life and have it abundantly"* (John 10:10). What then is the essence of the biblical Gospel?

GOD

The biblical Gospel begins with God, who is the Creator and Sustainer of all things. It has an exalted view of God, especially of His holiness. God is just and holy, and His wrath burns hot against sin and sinners. *"For the wrath of God is revealed from heaven against all ungodliness and unrighteousness of men, who by their unrighteousness suppress the truth"* (Rom.1:18). ; *"Whoever believes in the Son has eternal life; whoever does not obey the Son shall not see life, but the wrath of God remains on him"* (John 3:36).

MAN

The biblical Gospel holds that God made man for Himself so that man could find purpose and fulfillment in fellowship with God. *"For by him all things were created, in heaven and on earth, visible and invisible, whether thrones or dominions or rulers or authorities—all things were created through him and for him"* (Col. 1:16). However, because all men have fallen in Adam, they are sinners by nature and by choice. *"For all have sinned and fall short of the glory of God"* (Rom. 3:23). As sinners, men are enslaved to sin (even their wills are enslaved) and they are the objects of God's wrath. Men are in rebellion against God. Their sinful actions display their independence from God. They are enemies of the cross.

The biblical Gospel states that because man has rebelled and turned from God,

27

he is spiritually separated from God. *"But your iniquities have made a separation between you and your God, and your sins have hidden his face from you so that he does not hear"* (Isa. 59:2). The result of sin is spiritual death. *"For the wages of sin is death, but the free gift of God is eternal life in Christ Jesus our Lord"* (Rom. 6:23). This condition of being physically alive and spiritually dead, if not rectified, will result in eternal judgment at physical death. *"And just as it is appointed for man to die once, and after that comes judgment"* (Heb. 9:27). *"Then he will say to those on his left, 'Depart from me, you cursed, into the eternal fire prepared for the devil and his angels'"* (Matt. 25:41).

CHRIST

The biblical Gospel says that sinners cannot save themselves, but God through the death of Christ does save sinners and restores the broken fellowship. *"But God shows his love for us in that while we were still sinners, Christ died for us"* (Rom. 5:8) *"Whom God put forward as a propitiation by his blood, to be received by faith. This was to show God's righteousness, because in his divine forbearance he had passed over former sins. It was to show his righteousness at the present time, so that he might be just and the justifier of the one who has faith in Jesus"* (Rom. 3:25-26). Christ in His death procured and secured salvation for sinners. God came in the flesh and made a perfect atonement for sin and sinners. It is at the cross that we see God's great love for a sinful race.

The biblical Gospel declares that after Christ's death for sin, He rose victorious over sin and death by a bodily resurrection from the dead. *"It will be counted to us who believe in him who raised from the dead Jesus our Lord, who was delivered up for our trespasses and raised for our justification"* (Rom 4:24b-25). Christ is alive today to give men a new life of fellowship with God. *"The thief comes only to steal and kill and destroy. I came that they may have life and have it abundantly"* (John 10:10).

RESPONSE

The biblical Gospel says a person must recognize his condition before God as a sinner, he must repent (change his mind about God, Christ, and sin), and he must be willing to embark on a new lifestyle. *"The times of ignorance God overlooked, but now he commands all people everywhere to repent"* (Acts 17:30) *"From that time Jesus began to preach, saying, 'Repent, for the kingdom of heaven is at hand'"* (Matt. 4:17). He must believe that Christ died for him so that he might be forgiven, and accept Christ as the Lord (God), Jesus (Savior), and Christ (Messiah). *"And they said, 'Believe in the Lord Jesus, and you will be saved, you and your household'"* (Acts 16:31). He must receive Christ as Savior and Lord with the intent of obeying Him, and this receiving of Christ is done by an act of faith whereby Christ is invited into the life. *"But to all who did receive him, who believed in his name, he gave the right to become children of God"* (John 1:12).

The biblical Gospel teaches deliverance from sin and hell through an all sufficient Savior, Jesus Christ. This deliverance comes through a supernatural calling and a new birth which is caused solely by God.

How can this theology be translated into life? Simply, he must repent and believe. He must forsake his sins and then go on to forsake himself. Let him cover nothing, defend nothing, excuse nothing. Let him not seek to make terms with God, but let him bow his head before the stroke of God's stern displeasure and acknowledge himself worthy to die. Having done this let him gaze with simple trust upon the risen Savior, and from Him will come life and rebirth and cleansing and power. The Cross that ended the earthly life of Jesus now puts an end to the sinner; and the power that raised Christ from the dead now raises him to a new life along with Christ. (Tozer)

THE NEW GOSPEL

A new Gospel, which in some ways closely resembles the biblical Gospel, is being preached today by many evangelicals. Many of the same terms are used, and so one may think the new Gospel is quite biblical. It is not what the new Gospel says but what it does not say that is dangerous. The new Gospel is the product of three things: 1) man's sinful heart, which refuses to recognize the total depravity of man and the sovereignty of God; 2) a Western culture which is humanistic to the core and thus man-centered; and 3) the measuring of success in Christian undertakings by size and numbers.

THE NEW GOSPEL IS MAN-CENTERED

The new Gospel begins everything with man, so that he becomes autonomous (self-containing). Man becomes the cause of his own salvation. Any salvation that begins or ends with man is not a biblical Gospel but an erroneous Gospel, for salvation is of God. The biblical Gospel regards faith as part of God's gift of salvation, while the new Gospel regards faith as man's own contribution to salvation. One view gives all the glory to God for saving sinners; the other divides the glory between God and man.

THE NEW GOSPEL LACKS BIBLICAL CONTENT

The new Gospel has many biblical concepts, but it leaves out or plays down some important aspects of the true Gospel in order to make it palatable to the unsaved. The new Gospel stresses heavily the love of God, but key concepts such as sin, judgment, hell, and repentance are neglected. God's holiness, justice, righteousness, and sovereignty are played down, and the new Gospel does everything possible to take the harshness out of Christianity so as to make the Christian message acceptable to men. Advocates of the new Gospel stress the positives and not the negatives of the Christian faith. Some call this "side-door evangelism" or "easy believism" because anything offensive is taken out of the Gospel.

Yet there is an offense to the biblical Gospel. There must be, if unsaved men are going to face up to the reality of sin, judgment, and eternal punishment.

> *For the word of the cross is folly to those who are perishing, but to us who are being saved it is the power of God. ... But we preach Christ crucified, a stumbling block to Jews and folly to Gentiles, but to those who are called, both Jews and Greeks, Christ the power of God and the wisdom of God. (1 Cor. 1:18, 23-24)*

Are we honest with the non-Christian when we fail to tell him the bad news of sin, separation, judgment, and perdition before we tell him the good news that Christ came to save sinners? Why do Christians fail to tell the bleak side of the Gospel? It is because they are interested in numbers alone, or because they do not like to be rejected. They water down, sugarcoat, and compromise the Gospel to see people make professions of faith, even though many of these people have never really repented of sin and turned wholly to Jesus Christ for salvation.

I have heard earnest Christians say to unbelievers, "You do not have to believe the heathen are lost, or in original sin, or the literalness of hell to be saved. Just trust Jesus and everything will be all right. Doctrine is not important and Jesus will teach you what you need to know." So the person makes some kind of superficial decision and profession of faith in Christ, and perhaps later faces the question of a literal hell or original sin and rejects them because he was told it was not important for salvation. Consequently, the person goes on believing and propagating a false Gospel.

The real issue is: Is it more important to please God or man in evangelism? To sacrifice Gospel content for the sake of numbers is a great sin before God, for there is no true Gospel without its doctrinal substructure.

> *For am I now seeking the approval of man, or of God? Or am I trying to please man? If I were still trying to please man, I would not be a servant of Christ. (Gal. 1:10)*

> *But just as we have been approved by God to be entrusted with the gospel, so we speak, not to please man, but to please God who tests our hearts. (1 Thess. 2:4)*

Every Christian will one day give an account to Christ as to whether he propagated the biblical Gospel for the glory of God.

THE NEW GOSPEL PRESENTS A WEAK GOD

The biblical Gospel is that a sovereign God saves sinners on the basis of Christ's death by means of faith in Christ as Lord and Savior; that is, God saves and not men. The new Gospel, however, presents a God who is trying His hardest to save all men but He cannot do it, for the wills of men stop a sovereign God from saving.

Fifteen hundred years ago, Pelagius was condemned as a heretic for making the following statement. "All therefore have free will to sin and not to sin … it is not free will if it requires the aid of God, because everyone has it within the power of his own will to do anything or not to do anything." A well-known evangelist of today has said, "One thing that God cannot do is save men against their wills. If they were not free to say 'no,' then they are not free to say 'yes.' In the twenty-first century, hardly anyone raises an eyebrow at this kind of a statement because most Christians have a very humanistic God who cannot work until man first works.

Thus, we appeal to men as if they all had the ability to receive Christ at any time; we speak of His redeeming work as if He had done no more by dying than make it possible for us to save ourselves by believing; we speak of God's love as if it were no more than a general willingness to receive any who will turn and trust; and we depict the Father and the Son, not as sovereignly active in drawing sinners to themselves, but as waiting in quiet impotence "at the door of our hearts" for us to let them in. It is undeniable that this is how we preach; perhaps this is what we really believe. But it needs to be said with emphasis that this set of twisted half-truths is something other than the Biblical Gospel. The Bible is against us when we preach in this way; and the fact that such preaching has become almost standard practice among us only shows how urgent it is that we should review this matter. (J. I. Packer)

THE NEW GOSPEL SUBTLY TEACHES WORKS

The new Gospel teaches that God has done everything He can do to save a man, and now the rest is up to man as to whether he will receive Christ. This states that man's act of faith by the will is totally independent of God, and thus it would be a work. The Bible, however, says that one's total salvation is of God, even one's faith, because salvation is apart from any human work or act. *"For by grace you have been saved through faith. And this is not your own doing; it is the gift of God, not a result of works, so that no one may boast"* (Eph. 2:8-9). There must always be a stress on supernaturalism in evangelism, for it is God who saves men by His grace.

THE NEW GOSPEL IS EXPERIENCE ORIENTED

The new Gospel is presented in such a way that men will see the benefits of salvation they will receive from becoming a Christian. It presents Christ as one who will make a person more successful, a better athlete, a happy person, or someone free from problems. Christ is not declared as the Savior from sin and judgment but as the "joy-giver"; that is, as one who can give joy, peace, and happiness to people. The essence of the new Gospel is to present Christ in terms of how He can please and satisfy men rather than how men can please and satisfy God. *"Finally, then, brothers, we ask and urge you in the Lord Jesus, that as you received from us how you ought to live and to please God, just as you are doing, that you do so more and more"* (1 Thess. 4:1). The goal of Christianity is not to obtain the maximum satisfaction for oneself, but to please God. Obedience to God is more important then experience; yet those who obey God will experience God. *"'Whoever has my commandments and keeps them, he it is who loves me. And he who loves me will be loved by my Father, and I will love him and manifest myself to him'"* (John 14:21).

There are many side benefits to a person who trusts in Christ as Lord and Savior. There will be peace, security, stability, purpose, and joy to some degree, but no one should come to Christ just to have these experiences. Men lack peace, security, stability, purpose, and joy because of sin. Sin has separated them from God. Therefore, they must come to Christ to deal with their sin problem first; then, God will progressively bring the byproducts of joy and peace.

One way of stating the difference between the new Gospel and the old Gospel is to say that the new is too much concerned with being "helpful" to man to bring peace, comfort, happiness, satisfaction and too little concerned with glorifying God. The old Gospel was "helpful" too more so, indeed, than the new but less intentionally and more incidentally, for its first concern is always to give glory to God. But in the new Gospel the center of reference is man. This is just to say that the old Gospel was religious in a way that the new Gospel is not. Whereas the chief aim of the old was to teach men to worship God, the concern of the new seems limited to making them feel better. The subject of the old Gospel was God and His ways with men; the subject of the new is man and the help that God gives him. There is a world of difference. The whole perspective and emphasis of Gospel preaching has changed. From this change of interest has sprung a change of content, for the new Gospel has in effect reformulated the biblical message in the supposed interests of "helpfulness." Accordingly, the themes of man's natural inability to believe, of God's free election being the ultimate cause of salvation, and of Christ dying specifically for His sheep, are not preached. These doctrines, it would be said, are not "helpful"; they would drive sinners to despair, by suggesting to them that it is not in their own power to be saved through Christ. (Packer)

THE NEW GOSPEL IS DECISION-CENTERED

The chief end of the new Gospel is to get men to make a decision, a commitment to Christ, at any cost. This is often done by the use of gimmicks, emotional appeals, and pressure tactics. Decision-centered evangelism has resulted in many professions of faith in Christ, but this often is not true salvation. Many evangelicals are in the numbers game, and much of the "success" of their ministry is measured by how many decisions they can get in a month or a year.

THE NEW GOSPEL HOLDS HANDS WITH THE WORLD

The new Gospel says that a person need not have a changed life and leave the world system with its godless philosophy, habits, attitudes, and ethics. The world is no longer presented as the Christian's enemy but as his friend. The new Gospel says that a person can have the world and Christ too, but this is not biblical.

> *Do not love the world or the things in the world. If anyone loves the world, the love of the Father is not in him. For all that is in the world— the desires of the flesh and the desires of the eyes and pride in possessions—is not from the Father but is from the world. And the world is passing away along with its desires, but whoever does the will of God abides forever. (1 John 2:15-17)*

The biblical Gospel teaches that salvation is a radical break with the old, unsaved life in Adam, and that there is a new and dynamic life in Christ. This new life in Christ makes demands on Christians to live under the Lordship of Christ. *"Whoever does not bear his own cross and come after me cannot be my disciple"* (Luke 14:27).

THE NEW GOSPEL IS SUBTLY TEACHING UNIVERSALISM

Most evangelicals do not think they are universalists (those who believe that all will be saved). They are not, but their inconsistent theology leads to universalism. Universalism is the logical direction from their teaching that "God loves all and Christ died for all and the Holy Spirit is trying to save all." There is a progression downward as one accepts the new Gospel theology. First, a God of love would not judge the heathen who have never heard the Gospel. Second, if God is really love, He will not judge people who are sincere about religion (any religion) or life, but He may judge the really bad people. Third, if God loves everyone, He will accept them, good or bad, and will not send anyone to hell.

But if we start by affirming that God has a saving love for all, and Christ died a saving death for all, and yet balk at becoming universalists, there is nothing else that we can say. Let us be clear on what we have done when we have put the matter in this fashion. We have not exalted grace and the cross; we have cheapened them. … We have flattered impenitent sinners by assuring them that it is in their power to repent and believe, though God cannot make them do it. Perhaps we have also trivialized faith and repentance in order to make this assurance plausible ("It's very simple just open your heart to the Lord …"). Certainly, we have effectively denied God's sovereignty and undermined the basic conviction of religion that man is always in God's hands. In truth, we have lost a great deal. And it is, perhaps, no wonder that our preaching begets so little reverence and humility, and that our professed converts are so selfconfident and so deficient in selfknowledge, and in the good works which Scripture regards as the fruit of true repentance. (Packer)

33

It may well be that a watered-down, compromised, and unbiblical Christianity may become the religion of the state in America. All religions will be able to rally under the banner of Christianity, but it will in no way be a biblical Christianity. This may set the stage for the Antichrist, whose Gospel will deceive multitudes.

CONCLUSION

What is the Gospel? God, the Creator of the universe, is holy and just, and His wrath burns hot against sin. Man was made by God for fellowship with God but has sinned and rebelled against God, choosing to go his own independent way. Therefore, he is separated from God and is spiritually dead. God must judge the sinner because he sins. This is the bad news. The good news is that God has sent His Son, Jesus Christ, to die for sinners. Christ has made a complete and perfect salvation for sin and sinners in His death, and it is at the cross that we may see God's love manifested. Christ not only died for sinners, but He rose from the dead to give man a new life so he might come alive spiritually and have fellowship with God. This is the Gospel, the good news.

What then must the sinner do to be saved? He must recognize himself as a sinner, change his mind about Christ, and be willing to start a new life in Christ. He must then believe on the Lord Jesus Christ, accepting Him as the One who died for his sins and the One who was raised from the dead to give him new life. He must receive Christ by faith into his life, granting Him the right to rule and to make him the person He wants him to be.

QUESTIONS:

1. From what you have learned from this chapter and from your study of the Bible, how would you define the word "gospel"?
2. What aspects of the gospel are being neglected, even by Christians, in an attempt to make it more palatable to people?
3. How can you tell the difference between a God-centered gospel and a man-centered gospel? What difference does it make?
4. Prepare an outline of the important aspects of the gospel to share with someone this very week.

chapter 4:

grace

OBJECTIVES

- To know how the Bible defines "grace."
- To grasp clearly why grace is vital to our understanding of who God is and what God has done for us.
- To understand that grace is the basis for all aspects of our relationship with God.
- To be able to respond to objections to the idea that all is of grace.

> *Amazing grace, how sweet the sound,*
> *That saved a wretch like me!*
> *I once was lost, but now am found,*
> *Was blind but now I see.*

What did John Newton mean by amazing grace? What do we mean by grace? We are often so glib when we speak the wonderful word "grace." As Christians we have read the word "grace" in our Bibles hundreds of times; we have heard it taught in Sunday School and from the pulpit, and we have sung the word "grace" in our hymns. But what does it mean?

I am convinced that many Christians never understand the full meaning of grace because they do not understand the depth of their own sinfulness, nor do they see that grace is related to God's sovereign purposes in election and predestination. Do not misunderstand me; I think that all Christians know that God saved them through Christ in grace, but they do not understand that it was *all* of grace.

A few years ago, a man who had been a Christian for some time came to a biblical understanding of God's sovereign purposes in salvation. He said to me, "I have always believed in God's grace, but until recently, since I have come to believe in election and predestination, I did not understand the real meaning of grace. Now I understand that it is all of grace."

DEFINITION OF GRACE

There is no song or theological definition that can accurately convey to us the meaning of grace. It is a truth far beyond human comprehension. Neither the Old Testament nor the New Testament gives a definition of grace, nor does either try to explain the concept. However, the Bible does speak much about the grace of God. The Bible teaches that grace flows from the sovereign character of God, who is gracious in His acts.

The LORD, the LORD, a God merciful and gracious, slow to anger, and abounding in steadfast love and faithfulness, keeping steadfast love for thousands, forgiving iniquity and transgression and sin, but who will by no means clear the guilty. (Ex. 34:6-7)

The LORD is merciful and gracious, slow to anger and abounding in steadfast love. (Psa. 103:8)

The theological definition of grace is "unmerited favor." Grace is receiving something when we are not worthy. Grace is the free bestowal of kindness on one who has absolutely no claim on it. Grace is the good pleasure of God that inclines Him to bestow benefits on the undeserving.

We will never come to a full understanding of God's grace in salvation until we understand the depths of our sin before we were converted to Christ. In our unsaved state, we had wrong thoughts and wrong acts toward the holy character and law of God. We were sinners in rebellion to God and enemies of God. We were going our own independent way and deserved absolutely nothing from God but eternal perdition. God owed no obligation to us as His creatures. If He chose to shower kindness on us in Christ, it was purely a gracious act of God. The most important aspect of grace is that it is freely given by God. It cannot be bought, earned or won by man, or it would cease to be grace. Grace cannot be fully understood until a person realizes that he is a sinner and totally depraved.

USAGE OF GRACE

When we examine how the Bible uses the word "grace" as it relates to a sinner's conversion, we discover that a Christian's salvation is purely by God's sovereign grace. Not one person who is saved deserves it, and, if he is saved, it is because God has graciously bestowed this salvation on him.

GRACE CAUSED OUR SALVATION

For by grace you have been saved through faith. And this is not your own doing; it is the gift of God, not a result of works, so that no one may boast. (Eph. 2:8-9)

The Bible makes it clear that God's grace is the first and final cause of salvation. The cause is grace and the means of appropriating salvation is through faith in the Lord Jesus Christ. Salvation is all of grace and yet it is not apart from faith.

Over and over again the Bible declares that salvation is not of human works or acts but is of God's sovereign grace. *"But if it is by grace, it is no longer on the basis of works; otherwise grace would no longer be grace"* (Rom. 11:6). *"That is why it depends on faith, in order that the promise may rest on grace and be guaranteed to all his offspring—not only to the adherent of the law but also to the one who shares the faith of Abraham, who is the father of us all"* (Rom. 4:16).

Salvation is not gained by anything but God's pure grace. One cannot buy salvation, or work, weep or beg for it. It is a free gift from God.

Sovereign grace o'er sin abounding,
Ransomed souls, the tidings swell;
Tis a deep that knows no sounding
Who its breadth or length can tell?
On its glories,
On its glories,
Let my soul forever dwell.
John Kent (1766-1843)

GRACE IS THE BASIS FOR ELECTION

So too at the present time there is a remnant, chosen by grace. (Rom. 11:5)

God elects or chooses men to salvation because He is a gracious God. No human being deserves to be chosen by God.

GRACE IS RELATED TO PREDESTINATION

He predestined us for adoption through Jesus Christ, according to the purpose of his will, to the praise of his glorious grace, with which he has blessed us in the Beloved. (Eph 1:5-6)

Christians have been predestined to be adopted into God's family because God graciously moves on us to make us His people.

Perhaps now you are getting a clearer picture about grace. Now you can sing the hymn "At Calvary" with new meaning:

O, the love that drew salvation's plan!
O, the grace that brought it down to man!
O, the mighty gulf that God did span
At Calvary!

GRACE PROMPTED OUR CALL TO SALVATION

God] saved us and called us to a holy calling, not because of our
works but because of his own purpose and grace, which he gave us
in Christ Jesus before the ages began. (2 Tim. 1:9)

It was God's pure and sovereign grace that gave us an effective call to salvation in Christ Jesus. God called us to Himself through Christ because He willed to save us when we deserved nothing from God but hell. Do we really believe the words of the song "Saved by grace alone! This is all my plea!" (Philip Doddridge, 1702-1751).

GRACE IS THE SOURCE FOR OUR JUSTIFICATION

Sinners] are justified by his grace as a gift, through the redemp-
tion that is in Christ Jesus. (Rom. 3:24)

Christians are justified (declared righteous before God) by free grace from God. There was absolutely no cause in us as sinners for God to justify us. This verse, which is part of the inspired Bible, tells us clearly that grace is free and sovereign. Grace is free in that God freely gives it to men in Christ without any conditions whatsoever. If there were any conditions, then it would not be free. Free grace alone can save a person from sin and hell. Grace is sovereign in that God bestows His free grace on those He pleases.

Let us praise God that He has been pleased to justify some, for He was in no way obligated to save any rebellious sinner who willfully chooses to go against Christ and His kingdom. Let us remember that those God justifies are those whom He graciously decided to save for His own glory.

GRACE IS THE ROOT OF TRUE SAVING FAITH

And when he wished to cross to Achaia, the brothers encouraged him and wrote to the disciples to welcome him. When he arrived, he greatly helped those who through grace had believed. (Acts 18:27)

The most common misunderstanding of grace is as it relates to man's response in faith to Christ. The objectors to sovereign grace will say, "It is true that salvation is by grace but it is conditioned on the free will of man, for man must believe before God will move in His grace to save." Let's think through that statement for a moment. While it is true that no one will ever be saved apart from faith in Jesus Christ, faith is not the cause of salvation. Grace is the cause of salvation which includes faith in Jesus Christ. God's sovereign grace allowed us to believe in Christ. Had not God been gracious to us, we would yet be in our sins and rejecters of Christ. The Scriptures are clear, for we are saved *"By grace . . . through faith"* (Eph. 2:8).

Recently I heard a well-known radio Bible teacher say he could not understand the common definition of grace, which is "unmerited favor from God." He said he could understand his own definition, which is "God giving and my receiving." He stressed the words "my receiving" but this de-emphasizes grace. Even "my receiving" is caused by God's grace.

CONFUSION ABOUT GRACE

It is my conviction that every true child of God through faith in Christ Jesus knows he has been saved by grace. He knows it in his heart even though he may deny it in his head. Most Christians have a practice that is far superior to their theological understanding. For instance, all Christians thank God for their salvation and not one would claim he saved himself. Christians know intuitively from the Holy Spirit that God's grace saved them, even though they may be confused about how this fits with man's response to Christ.

Every Christian, whether free will or free grace oriented, knows that God did a previous work of grace in him before he trusted in Christ. The problem always lies in the place of the human will in response to Christ. Did that response initiate from God or man? Notice the following poem:

O my God, what must I do?
Thou alone the way canst show;
Thou canst save me in this hour,
I have neither will nor power;
God, if over all thou art,
Greater than my sinful heart,
All thy power on me be shown,
Take away the heart of stone.

Take away my darling sin,
Make me willing to be clean;
Make me willing to receive
All Thy goodness waits to give:
Force me, Lord, with all to part,
Tear these idols from my heart;
Now thy love almighty show,
Make e'en me a creature new.

Jesus, mighty to renew,
Work in me to will and do;
Turn my nature's rapid tide,
Stem the torrent of my pride;
Stop the whirlwind of my will;
Speak, and bid the sun stand still;
Now thy love almighty show,
Make e'en me a creature new.

Arm of God, thy strength put on,
Bow the heavens, and come down;
All my unbelief o'erthrow,
Lay the' aspiring mountain low;
Conquer thy worst foe in me,
Get thyself the victory;
Save the vilest of the race,
Force me to be saved by grace.
(Charles Wesley, 1707-1788)

Notice how this writer says things such as "Thou canst save me" and "I have neither will nor power." Over and over again he says, "Make me willing." Then he says, "Force me to be saved by grace." This sounds like the writings of some fatalist or hyper-determinist, but they are the words of Charles Wesley, a staunch free-willer. Why these strong words? Because in his heart and practice, Wesley knew God had to work sovereignly before a person could be saved. This is the position of a person who believes in sovereign grace—that God must make a man willing by His grace to respond to Christ and be saved.

THEOLOGICAL PROBLEMS CONNECTED WITH GRACE

Doesn't the Bible Teach that God Gives Grace to Everyone?

It is interesting to observe that "grace" is never mentioned in connection with all mankind but always in relation to the true people of God. There is no such thing as universal saving grace, only particular grace to all who are true believers in Christ.

The astute Bible student may object to my statement that grace is related only to true Christians in light of Titus 2:11, which says, "For the grace of God that bringeth salvation hath appeared to all men" (KJV). The objector says, "See, grace has appeared to all men, so all men must have grace enough to exercise free will and trust Christ." One answer to the belief that all men have grace is found in a proper translation of Titus 2:11. This could be translated, "For the grace of God that bringeth salvation hath appeared for all men." This translation tells us that Christ's salvation is for all men if all men will lay hold of it by faith. A second possible answer is to put Titus 2:11 in context, where it is obvious that it is referring to believers. The "all men" refers to all who believe in Christ, for Titus 2:12 says grace is, "training us [Christians] to renounce ungodliness and worldly passions, and to live self-controlled, upright, and godly lives in the present age." Therefore, we may conclude that God does not give grace to everyone, but He gives grace to whom He pleases in Christ Jesus.

Does Sovereign Grace Destroy One's Desire to Live a Godly Life?

Some Christians illogically reason that if God has a plan, then there is no need to try to live the Christian life — because what will be, will be. That is faulty reasoning. The fact that God has a plan does not destroy any part of human responsibility. Responsibility is the divinely appointed means for attaining God's sovereign ends. God has purposed that a man shall reap, but He has also purposed that a man shall sow.

A farmer does not stop sowing seed just because he is sure there will be a crop. On the contrary, he plants *because* he is sure there will be a crop! Do we stop giving people food when they are hungry or medicine when they are sick because we know that God has appointed the time and manner of every man's death? Absolutely not! We use all the means at our disposal to prolong life, knowing full well that God will take people in death at the appointed hour.

The Christian is guaranteed great success from God if he will avail himself of the means of faith, obedience, and perseverance. The Christian knows that ultimately he will win the battle over sin and death. Both reason and experience teach us that the greater one's hope of success, the stronger becomes the motive to action. The person who is sure of success in the use of appropriate means has the strongest incentive to work. The Christian, then, who has before him the definite commands of God, and the promise that the work of those who obediently and reverently avail themselves of appointed means shall be blessed and successful, has the highest possible motive for action. Christians have already positionally won the war against sin and death, but they are still fighting mop-up battles until the war is actually over, when they receive their new bodies.

A belief in sovereign grace gives the Christian great confidence. He begins to feel that he is an instrument of destiny. A person who regards himself as predestined to achieve some great goal acts with dynamic force and discipline to attain it. He is not divided by doubts or weakened by scruples or fears. He believes fully that he will succeed, and that belief is the greatest assistance to success. Great men of history such as Julius Caesar, Attila the Hun, Napoleon Bonaparte, and many others all felt they were men of destiny. The Christian is a person of destiny, and a thorough understanding of this destiny steels his nerves, redoubles his courage, and fixes his purpose on glorifying Christ on this earth, knowing that with faith, obedience, and perseverance, he will succeed.

The same grace that saved us is working sanctification in us as Christians (Phil. 1:6; 2:12-13). We work because God is at work in us. God began our salvation by grace and continues it by grace (Col. 2:6). We need as much or more grace for sanctification (Christian living) as we do for initial salvation.

EXAMPLE OF GRACE

For I am the least of the apostles, unworthy to be called an apostle, because I persecuted the church of God. But by the grace of God I am what I am, and his grace toward me was not in vain. On the contrary, I worked harder than any of them, though it was not I, but the grace of God that is with me.   (1 Cor. 15:9-10)

The Apostle Paul is the supreme example of one who was touched by and overwhelmed with God's grace. Paul before his conversion was a hater of Christ and persecuted the followers of Christ in the name of God (Acts 8:1-3). On the road to Damascus, God intervened in Paul's life, and he was converted to Christ (Acts 9:1-18). God moved in sovereign grace to save Paul, so as to break his will that he might follow the Savior. There was never a question in Paul's mind that God chose him to salvation and service.

For I am the least of the apostles, unworthy to be called an apostle, because I persecuted the church of God. (1 Cor. 15:9)

No one had to tell Paul he was a sinner. He knew it. He had intentionally and intensely persecuted the church, the body of Christ. Because of this persecution, Paul called himself the "foremost" of sinners (1 Tim. 1:15), Paul before conversion was an enemy of God and in rebellion to God's moral law. He understood that he was totally depraved.

But by the grace of God I am what I am. (1 Cor. 15:9)

Paul knew too well that all he was and all that he had in Christ were due to the grace of God alone. Paul knew his salvation was of the Lord. He clearly understood that he did not seek and choose God, but that God chose and sought him. God gave Paul salvation, the forgiveness of sins, eternal life, position in His family, and even the faith to trust in Christ. Paul deserved nothing from God but punishment, but God in His sovereign grace saved Paul and made him a great man of faith. Why did God take a rotten sinner like Paul and save and use him to the glory of God? I do not know! But I do know it was grace that saved Paul.

His grace toward me was not in vain. On the contrary, I worked harder than any of them, though it was not I, but the grace of God that is with me. (1 Cor. 15:10)

God's grace motivated Paul to great action for God. Out of deep appreciation for his salvation, Paul worked diligently for Christ. Sovereign grace did not make Paul a cold, hard, critical fatalist, but it caused him to move out for God. Paul makes what seems to be a bragging statement, for he declares he labored more than the other apostles. He labored to the point of mental and physical exhaustion to bring the good news of Jesus Christ to sinners.

Though it was not I, but the grace of God that is with me. (1 Cor. 15:10)

Paul clarifies what may seem to be a boast, and says that it was the grace of God that allowed him to do what he did for Christ. Paul did nothing of himself, and it was all of the grace of God. The Apostle Paul found no room for human boasting because he understood much about God's sovereign grace.

Why don't Christians labor more for Christ? They do not appreciate their salvation. Why don't they appreciate salvation? Because they do not understand grace. Not until we understand that every phase and facet of our salvation is from God will we really grasp grace. There are two kinds of people who claim to believe in the doctrines of election and predestination to salvation—those who believe intellectually in election and predestination and those who have been deeply touched by sovereign grace. There is a world of difference between the two. Only those who experientially grasp sovereign grace can say, "But by the grace of God I am what I am."

CONCLUSION

Someone may say, "What if God will not grant me grace even if I want to trust Christ and be saved?" Friend, you would not even desire to be saved unless God was working in your heart to trust the Savior. God does grant grace to the elect sinner to believe that Christ died for his sins and was raised from the dead to declare him righteous. His responsibility is to trust Christ, and when he does he will realize that it was God's grace that enabled him to make the decision. God gives grace, but God does not exercise faith. It is our faith, not God's faith. It is our responsibility to believe. We must trust the Savior for ourselves, and God must grant grace for us to be saved. Great is the mystery of salvation, but oh, how wonderful it is!

QUESTIONS:

1. From what you have learned from this chapter and from your study of the Bible, what is the meaning of the word "grace"?
2. Why is it important to believe that salvation is all of grace and not of works? How does this affect your view of God, and the way you live your life?
3. Tell how grace works through the various aspects of salvation. This includes election, predestination, calling, justification, and any other aspect of salvation of which you are aware.
4. What would you say to someone who objects that sovereign grace would stifle a person's desire for a godly life?

chapter 5:

mercy

OBJECTIVES

- To know the meaning of "mercy" as used in the Bible.
- To grasp the importance of an understanding of mercy for knowing who God is and what He has done for you.
- To be able to explain the different aspects of God's mercy.
- To look to your own life for the differences that result from God's mercy.

Someone made this piercing statement, "We live in a world of despair." Men and women all about us are filled with suffering, misery, and futility. Even a humanist such as Henry David Thoreau saw this many years ago, as he wrote in *Walden*, "The mass of men lead lives of quiet desperation." In this age of pessimism, dejection, and despondency, men are crying out, "Are there any real answers to life? Is there any way out of the maze of meaninglessness? Is there anyone who really cares about man's plight and despair?" These are difficult questions, but I can assure you that if man looks to man for the answers, man will fall deeper into hopeless despair. The answer to man's plight is not found in man.

The answer to man's despair and desperation is not found in human wisdom, reasoning, or philosophy, but in God. I thank God that I can tell you without reservation that there is someone who cares. God cares because God is a God of mercy. God specializes in showing mercy to men whose hopes of life have been dashed on the rocks of reality.

> *"The LORD passed before him and proclaimed, 'The LORD, the LORD, a God merciful and gracious, slow to anger, and abounding in steadfast love and faithfulness'"* (Ex. 34:6). *"O give thanks unto the Lord; for he is good; for his mercy endureth forever"* (Ps. 136:1 KJV).

DEFINITION OF MERCY

Mercy is God's compassion or pity toward sinful men who are in misery and in need of divine help. Mercy differs from grace in that grace has reference to sinful man as *guilty*, while mercy has reference to sinful man as *miserable*.

Man lives a life of despair and desperation because he is a sinner who is in rebellion against God and who lives independent of God. Sinful man is trying his hardest to go in the opposite direction of where God wants him to go. His sinful, rebellious, independent, free spirit from God is what brings misery into his life. Sinful man is unhappy and unfulfilled. Misery may come as a result of gross sins such as drunkenness, murder, adultery, premarital sex, or homosexuality. Misery may also come to the soul of a man because of more subtle sins such as pride, envy, jealousy, lying, materialism, or hate. This misery comes often as one seeks to live a superficial, empty, two-faced, humdrum kind of existence, shoving God aside in his life because he does not want to be bothered by God-thoughts or be disturbed in his selfish life. However, because God is merciful, He is ready to relieve the misery of His fallen creatures. There is no relief for this misery apart from knowing God through Christ Jesus, the Lord.

St. Augustine said, "Thou hast made us for Thyself, O God, and our hearts are restless until they find their rest in Thee."

God always stands ready to place His mercy on a repentant sinner. We never have to wonder whether God will be merciful one day and not merciful the next. His boundless, immense, and overwhelming mercy stands ready always to dispense divine pity and compassion. This is why the Bible speaks of God's mercy [sometimes translated "steadfast love"] as "great" (1 Kings 3:6), "tender" (Luke 1:78), and "abundant" (1 Peter 1:3 KJV). God is the source of all mercy, and apart from Him there is no mercy for any person. This is why God is called "the Father of mercies" (2 Cor. 1:3).

CHARACTERISTICS OF MERCY

GOD'S MERCY IS INFINITE

God is an infinite fountain of mercy. There is no end to His mercy. He bestows infinite blessings on His own. The Bible says that God is *"plenteous [abundant] in mercy"* (Ps. 86:5 KJV) and *"rich in mercy"* (Eph. 2:4). It is impossible to exhaust God's reservoir of mercy, and there is always mercy enough for the person who avails himself of God's mercy.

GOD'S MERCY IS ETERNAL

God is eternal and His mercy is eternal. As long as God is God, He will be showing mercy on His creatures. *"But the mercy of the Lord is from everlasting to everlasting upon them that fear Him"* (Ps. 103:17 KJV).

God gives mercy to whom He desires, because God does as He pleases in heaven and on earth. *"And he said, 'I will make all my goodness pass before you and will proclaim before you my name "The LORD." And I will be gracious to whom I will be gracious, and will show mercy on whom I will show mercy'"* (Ex. 33:19). *"For he says to Moses, 'I will have mercy on whom I have mercy, and I will have compassion on whom I have compassion'"* (Rom. 9:15). *"So then he has mercy on whomever he wills, and he hardens whomever he wills"* (Rom. 9:18). Mercy is from God with no strings attached. It is free and sovereign. No man deserves mercy, because he is a polluted sinner. God is not obligated to any man, and no man has any claim on the mercy of God. To speak of men deserving the mercy of God is a contradiction, for mercy is free and no man deserves it. If God should show mercy to those who were worthy or deserving, He would show no mercy at all, for no man deserves anything from God. If any man receives mercy, it is by a sovereign act of God alone.

THE UNSAVED MAN AND GOD'S MERCY

For those who are without Christ and outside God's plan of salvation, there is particular special mercy from God that can bring them to salvation. This mercy is from God through Jesus. It is the great design of the Scriptures to represent God as merciful, for God delights in showing mercy to sinners. *"Who is a God like unto thee, that pardoneth iniquity, and passeth by transgression of the remnant of his heritage? He retaineth not his anger forever, because he delighteth in mercy"* (Micah 7:18 KJV).

It is by the pure mercy of God that He has not taken the rejecter of Christ and destroyed him in perdition. God's justice demands that He judge him for all eternity because he is a sinner in rebellion to a holy God.

> *And the Lord passed by before him, and proclaimed, The Lord, The Lord God, compassionate and gracious, longsuffering, and abundant in goodness and truth, Keeping mercy for thousands, forgiving iniquity and transgression and sin, and that will by no means clear the guilty; visiting the iniquity of the fathers upon the children, and upon the children's children, unto the third and to the fourth generation.* (Ex. 34:6-7 KJV)

God's mercy withholds the speedy execution of His justice. *"It is of the Lord's mercies that we are not consumed, because his compassions fail not"* (Lam. 3:22 KJV). The sinner's rebellion against God and His Son Jesus Christ continually provokes God to wrath, but why does He not strike the sinner dead and cast him into hell? It is not because He cannot, for He is armed with omnipotence, but His mercy is withholding judgment. He is granting mercy so the man may repent and turn to the living God through Christ.

The sinner may say, "I do not know whether God will forgive me if I trust Christ. How do I know if He will save me?" This is the devil's logic, for the Bible says that God is merciful and that He is ready to pardon any poor sinner who trusts Christ. *"But you are a God ready to forgive, gracious and merciful, slow to anger and abounding in steadfast love, and did not forsake them"* (Neh. 9:17).

He says, "I do not know whether God will forgive me, for my sins are too great." Wait a minute! God's arm is not short to save. *"Behold, the LORD's hand is not shortened, that it cannot save ..."* (Isa. 59:1). Is he any worse than the Apostle Paul before he was saved? Paul was guilty of self-righteousness, lying, and pride, and voted to put Christians to death, but he received mercy from God and was gloriously saved. *"Though formerly I was a blasphemer, persecutor, and insolent opponent. But I received mercy because I had acted ignorantly in unbelief"* (1 Tim. 1:13).

To the sinner I would say, "Do not let the immensity of your sins discourage you, for God's mercy can pardon all sins, great and small. God's mercy flows from an infinite fountain. Take the cup of faith and drink of the waters of mercy. God shows particular mercy to sinners, and this should encourage you to believe and find salvation." *"And let the one who is thirsty come; let the one who desires take the water of life without price"* (Rev. 22:17). Only unbelief keeps the stream of God's mercy from flowing to you. Humble yourself and cry out to God, *"God, be merciful to me, a sinner!"* (Luke 18:13).

THE SAVED MAN AND MERCY

I want to ask you a simple question, "Why are you saved?" Your immediate answer may be, "I am saved because I have trusted in Jesus Christ as my personal Lord and Savior." That is true, and you would never have been saved unless you trusted in Christ. Now I want to ask you another, more complex question, "Why is it you believed in Christ when others do not, seeing all men are totally depraved sinners before a holy God?" The only possible answer is that you have become a special object of God's sovereign, saving mercy. For reasons known only to God, He has made you a vessel of mercy. Remember, you are saved on account of God's mercy and for no other reason. *"He saved us, not because of works done by us in righteousness, but according to his own mercy, by the washing of regeneration and renewal of the Holy Spirit"* (Titus 3:5).

God was merciful to you when you were in your unsaved state, when you cared absolutely nothing about God's mercy. As sinners we were enemies of God, in unholy rebellion toward God. We walked according to the philosophies of this world. We were captives of the devil and children of wrath and disobedience. We deserved nothing but hell, but received rich mercy from God.

And you were dead in the trespasses and sins in which you once walked, following the course of this world, following the prince of the power of the air, the spirit that is now at work in the sons of disobedience—among whom we all once lived in the passions of our flesh, carrying out the desires of the body and the mind, and were by nature children of wrath, like the rest of mankind. But God, being rich in mercy, because of the great love with which he loved us, even when we were dead in our trespasses, made us alive together with Christ—by grace you have been saved—and raised us up with him and seated us with him in the heavenly places in Christ Jesus, so that in the coming ages he might show the immeasurable riches of his grace in kindness toward us in Christ Jesus. (Eph. 2:17)

God intervened in your life when you were in total opposition to Christ and His kingdom. God's rich mercy brought you to the Savior. Thank God that He is rich in mercy or you would be yet in your sins, lost and headed for a Christless eternity.

God saved you by His infinite mercy, and you are now a vessel of mercy and not a vessel of wrath.

What if God, desiring to show his wrath and to make known his power, has endured with much patience vessels of wrath prepared for destruction, in order to make known the riches of his glory for vessels of mercy, which he has prepared beforehand for glory— even us whom he has called, not from the Jews only but also from the Gentiles? (Rom. 9:22-24)

The believer in Jesus Christ is not a reprobate who is rejected of God. He is not a vessel of wrath if he has trusted in Christ. He is a vessel of mercy. He has been granted mercy and entrance into heaven when he deserved nothing from the hand of God but eternal wrath.

THE RESULTS OF RECEIVING GOD'S MERCY

GODLY LIVES

Because the Christian is a special object of God's sovereign, particular, saving mercy in Christ, what an incentive this should be to walk a holy life! He can evidence to himself and to others that he is a vessel of mercy. God not only saved the Christian by His mercy, but wants the Christian to experience His mercy every day as he serves Christ through faith and obedience. *"The steadfast love of the LORD never ceases; his mercies never come to an end; they are new every morning; great is your faithfulness"* (Lam. 3:22-23). God's mercy is available to all who worship

49

the true God through Christ. *"But the mercy of the Lord is from everlasting to everlasting upon them that fear him, and his righteousness unto children's children"* (Ps. 103:17 KJV). Think of it. We are an object of God's particular mercy. We can experience God's mercies in this life and will experience them throughout eternity future.

GODLY WORSHIP

Worship should always result from an understanding of sovereign mercy. I do not believe a person can worship God to the fullest extent without a clear understanding of sovereign mercy. Only as a person realizes that he was first touched by God's mercy, being delivered out of sin's misery, will he come to grasp how sovereign God is. He will then be seen as our sovereign God who rightly deserves our homage, submission, and obedience as His subjects.

In Romans 11 the Apostle Paul tells how God gave the Jews opportunity to embrace the Gospel, but they turned from the truth. Because the Jews rejected Christ, the plan of God was to have the Gospel go to the Gentiles. This whole procedure was God's purpose that He might show mercy on all His chosen people, whether Jews or Gentiles.

> *Just as you were at one time disobedient to God but now have received mercy because of their disobedience, so they too have now been disobedient in order that by the mercy shown to you they also may now receive mercy. For God has consigned all to disobedience, that he may have mercy on all. (Rom. 11:30-32)*

Understanding something of God's plan and His infinite mercy brought Paul to ecstasy in the worship of God.

> *Oh, the depth of the riches and wisdom and knowledge of God! How unsearchable are his judgments and how inscrutable his ways! "For who has known the mind of the Lord, or who has been his counselor?" "Or who has given a gift to him that he might be repaid?" For from him and through him and to him are all things. To him be glory forever. Amen. (Rom. 11:33-36)*

Could your worship of God be weak because you are lacking in your understanding of God's mercy that is manifested in Christ? Has it dawned on you that God picked you out of the mass of sinful humanity through the cross for Himself? He put His mercy on you when you deserved nothing but eternal judgment. God could have passed you by, but did not. You are a special object of God's sovereign mercy because He took pity on you when you were in sin. If this truth does not cause you to appreciate your salvation and worship God, nothing will!

CONCLUSION

God is merciful, and He takes pity on all sinners who come to Jesus Christ and drink freely of Him by faith. God delights to take miserable sinners and make them happy, fulfilled saints. *"For thou, Lord, art good, and ready to forgive; and plenteous in mercy unto all them that call upon thee"* (Ps. 86:5 KJV). We know that it was God who showed mercy to us, graciously calling us to Himself, and when the sovereign, omnipotent Lord calls, the sinner cannot resist. That is the mercy of God.

QUESTIONS:
1. From what you have learned from this chapter and from your study of the Bible, what is the meaning of the word "mercy"? How is it different from "grace"?
2. Why is it important to know that the Lord is a God of mercy?
3. Explain what it means that God's mercy is infinite, eternal, and sovereign.
4. What would you say to an unbeliever about how God's mercy should affect what he believes and how he lives?

chapter 6:

atonement

OBJECTIVES

- To know the meaning of "atonement" as pictured in the Bible.
- To study how the atonement is portrayed and predicted in the Old Testament.
- To understand your need for atonement, and how God met this need in Jesus Christ.
- To be able to tell others about Christ as the atoning sacrifice.

Do you have a hard time getting the whole Bible to fit together for you? Have you ever asked yourself what is the relationship of the Book of Leviticus to the Book of Hebrews, or the Book of Isaiah to the Gospel of John?

You can begin to put together all the parts of the Bible when you understand that there are three basic concepts that connect everything: (1) God's total sovereignty over the world from the time of Adam to the end, (2) God's kingdom rule on earth from the time of Adam to the end, and (3) the necessity of a substitutionary sacrifice (atonement) for sin through the shedding of blood, coupled with the acceptance of this sacrifice by grace through faith from the time of Adam to the end. From Genesis to Revelation, the Bible uses these concepts; when you begin to look for them, the entire Bible will fit together for you.

The Bible focuses on the centrality of the cross. The death of Christ is the scarlet thread that weaves through the whole Bible. Both the Old Testament and the New Testament point to the perfect sacrifice of Christ for sin and sinners. The Old Testament looks forward to the cross. The New Testament looks back to the cross. The Old Testament speaks throughout of Jesus Christ and His death for sin, and Christ rebuked two disciples on the road to Emmaus for not seeing and understanding this essence of the Old Testament Scriptures.

And he said to them, "O foolish ones, and slow of heart to believe all that the prophets have spoken! Was it not necessary that the Christ should suffer these things and enter into his glory?" And beginning with Moses and all the Prophets, he interpreted to them in all the Scriptures the things concerning himself. (Luke 24:25-27)

These disciples were rebuked because they did not understand the basic nature and importance of atonement. Today also, even though men have the inspired Scriptures that speak to the atonement, they either will not study them or they are slow of heart to believe them.

DEFINITION OF ATONEMENT

The word "atonement" is found only in the Old Testament, and it means "a covering for sins." The Old Testament uses the word many times in connection with the shedding of blood and the forgiveness of sins.

If the whole congregation of Israel sins unintentionally and the thing is hidden from the eyes of the assembly, and they do any one of the things that by the LORD's commandments ought not to be done, and they realize their guilt, when the sin which they have committed becomes known, the assembly shall offer a bull from the herd for a sin offering and bring it in front of the tent of meeting. And the elders of the congregation shall lay their hands on the head of the bull before the LORD, and the bull shall be killed before the LORD. Then the anointed priest shall bring some of the blood of the bull into the tent of meeting, and the priest shall dip his finger in the blood and sprinkle it seven times before the LORD in front of the veil. And he shall put some of the blood on the horns of the altar that is in the tent of meeting before the LORD, and the rest of the blood he shall pour out at the base of the altar of burnt offering that is at the entrance of the tent of meeting. And all its fat he shall take from it and burn on the altar. Thus shall he do with the bull. As he did with the bull of the sin offering, so shall he do with this. And the priest shall make atonement for them, and they shall be forgiven. (Lev. 4:13-20)

One's sins could be forgiven in the Old Testament through the death of a sacrificial animal and the shedding of its blood.

The word "atonement" is not found in the New Testament. The King James Version does use the word in Romans 5:11 where it says that through Christ "we have received the atonement." However, the Greek word here should be translated "reconciliation." But just because the word is not used in the New Testament, that does not mean the concept is absent there. The concept of atonement is taught in the words "redemption," "propitiation," and "reconciliation" as they relate to the death of Christ. Atonement, then, as it is used in a theological sense, refers to everything accomplished by Christ through His complete and perfect work on the cross.

The basic concept of atonement in both the Old Testament and the New Testament is that of substitution. God substitutes a pure animal or a perfect man on behalf of sinful men. God accepts something in the place of man's death for his own sin.

THE NEED FOR ATONEMENT

Why does a person need atonement for sin? Why does he need a substitutionary sacrifice and a covering of his sins by the shedding of blood? Only for one reason: he is a sinner! All men are sinners and separated from a holy God. *"For all have sinned and fall short of the glory of God . . . ."* (Rom. 3:23). All men are guilty before a holy God and must pay the penalty for their sins. *"For the wages of sin is death . . . ."* (Rom. 6:23). All men are in line for judgment because of the penalty and curse of sin.

Man has no way of his own to free himself from the penalty of sin, or to remove the guilt of sin from his soul. Man is in a hopeless, helpless, and deplorable condition because of his total depravity – his inability to respond in obedience to God. Except that God make atonement for a sinner, the sinner shall perish in his sins. Unless a person sees himself as a sinner, he will have no need for atonement. *"And when Jesus heard it, he said to them, 'Those who are well have no need of a physician, but those who are sick. I came not to call the righteous, but sinners'"* (Mark 2:17).

ATONEMENT IN THE OLD TESTAMENT

The Old Testament sacrificial system was set forth by God to remind men that forgiveness of sins is by the shedding of blood alone. *"Indeed, under the law almost everything is purified with blood, and without the shedding of blood there is no forgiveness of sins"* (Heb. 9:22). Every time a person in the Old Testament era offered a sacrifice, it was supposed to bring to his attention that salvation is by grace through faith on the basis of the shedding of blood. These animal sacrifices did not actually save those who offered them, *"For it is impossible for the blood of bulls and goats to take away sins"* (Heb. 10:4); they merely covered the sins until God's ultimate sacrifice and sin-bearer should enter this world—Jesus Christ: *"For God so loved the world, that he gave his only Son, that whoever believes in him should not perish but have eternal life"* (John 3:16).

All the animal sacrifices of the Old Testament were designed to point forward to Christ, the Messiah, who was God's perfect sacrifice for sin and sinners.

The first sacrifice mentioned in the Bible was made for Adam and Eve. Adam and Eve sinned, but God made a provision for their sin. God killed an animal (shed its blood) and made coats of skin to cover them: *"And the LORD God made for Adam and for his wife garments of skins and clothed them"* (Gen. 3:21). This is a substitution in type—the death of the animal is accepted in place of the deaths of Adam and Eve.

The right way of sacrifice can be seen early in the history of man, with Abel and Cain. Cain brought a sacrifice of vegetables to God, and Abel brought an animal sacrifice.

> *In the course of time Cain brought to the LORD an offering of the fruit of the ground, and Abel also brought of the firstborn of his flock and of their fat portions. And the LORD had regard for Abel and his offering, but for Cain and his offering he had no regard.*
> *(Gen. 4:35)*

God accepted Abel's sacrifice but rejected Cain's. Why? God accepts only the substitutionary death of another through the shedding of blood.

God made animal sacrifices a divine ordinance for the nation of Israel, and the whole Levitical sacrificial system pointed to the necessity of a substitution through the shedding of blood. When a Jew sinned, he took a lamb or bull without blemish to the priest, who would lay his hands on the animal and identify the sins of the person with this animal. Then the animal would be slain and roasted on the Brazen Altar of Sacrifice. The blood of the animal would then be sprinkled on the doorway of the Holy Place of the Tabernacle (Lev. 1:35).

Every Jew knew that forgiveness of sins was by the shedding of blood. The Jews had this sacrificial system until 70 AD, when Jerusalem was plundered and captured by Titus and the Roman armies. God has not allowed the Jews to have a sacrificial system since. Why? Because the Messiah has come and offered Himself up as the Lamb of God for sin. There is no longer any need for a sacrificial system to cover sin because the ultimate sacrifice for sin has been made by Christ.

The Old Testament prophesied the death of Christ, pointing to the ultimate atonement for sin. Christ's death was spoken of 800 years before it occurred:

Surely he has borne our griefs and carried our sorrows;
yet we esteemed him stricken, smitten by God, and afflicted.
But he was wounded for our transgressions; he was crushed
for our iniquities;
upon him was the chastisement that brought us peace,
and with his stripes we are healed.
All we like sheep have gone astray;
we have turned every one to his own way;
and the LORD has laid on him the iniquity of us all. ...
Yet it was the will of the LORD to crush him;
he has put him to grief;
when his soul makes an offering for sin,
he shall see his offspring; he shall prolong his days;
the will of the LORD shall prosper in his hand.
Out of the anguish of his soul he shall see and be satisfied;
by his knowledge shall the righteous one, my servant,
make many to be accounted righteous,
and he shall bear their iniquities. (Isa. 53:46, 10-11)

Hundreds of years before anything was known about Roman crucifixion, the Holy Spirit recorded Christ's death through crucifixion for sin:

My God, my God, why have you forsaken me?
Why are you so far from saving me, from the words of my groaning?
O my God, I cry by day, but you do not answer,
and by night, but I find no rest. ... But I am a worm and not a man,
scorned by mankind and despised by the people.
All who see me mock me;
they make mouths at me; they wag their heads;
"He trusts in the LORD; let him deliver him;
let him rescue him, for he delights in him!" ... I am poured out like water,
and all my bones are out of joint;
my heart is like wax;
it is melted within my breast;
my strength is dried up like a potsherd,
and my tongue sticks to my jaws;
you lay me in the dust of death. ...

For dogs encompass me;
a company of evildoers encircles me;
they have pierced my hands and feet—
I can count all my bones—
they stare and gloat over me;
they divide my garments among them,
and for my clothing they cast lots. (Psa. 22:1-2, 6-8, 14-18)

It is obvious that Christ's death was known in the Old Testament not only by sacrificial type, but also by the sure word of prophecy.

CHRIST'S PREDICTION OF ATONEMENT

When God sent Jesus Christ into this world, it was for the primary purpose of saving a people. God's love sent Christ to be a sacrifice for sin. *"For God so loved the world, that he gave his only Son, that whoever believes in him should not perish but have eternal life"* (John 3:16). Christ told His disciples that He must suffer and die. *"And he began to teach them that the Son of Man must suffer many things and be rejected by the elders and the chief priests and the scribes and be killed, and after three days rise again"* (Mark 8:31). Christ clearly knew He had an appointed hour to die for the sins of man, and His humanity shrank back from this time:

> *"Now is my soul troubled. And what shall I say? 'Father, save me from this hour'? But for this purpose I have come to this hour." ... When Jesus had spoken these words, he lifted up his eyes to heaven, and said, "Father, the hour has come; glorify your Son that the Son may glorify you ..." (John 12:27; 17:1-2)*

Christ made no attempt to avoid being taken by the Roman authorities, for He knew He had an appointed hour to die for sin.

> *Then Jesus said to him, "Put your sword back into its place. For all who take the sword will perish by the sword. Do you think that I cannot appeal to my Father, and he will at once send me more than twelve legions of angels? But how then should the Scriptures be fulfilled, that it must be so?" (Matt. 26:52-54)*

Christ had to die! There was no other way for God to bring sinful men to Himself. Without the shedding of blood, there can be no salvation. Christ had to make atonement to save God's people.

Atonement could be made only by the shedding of blood. There is no atonement apart from the death of Christ, who shed His perfect, sinless blood for sin and sinners. Take the blood out of Christianity and you have no atonement. If there is no atonement, then there is no need for Christianity. *"We have now been justified by his blood ..."* (Rom. 5:9). "In him we have redemption through his blood, the forgiveness of our trespasses ..." (Eph. 1:7). *"Making peace by the blood of his cross"* (Col. 1:20). *"He entered once for all into the holy places, not by means of the blood of goats and calves but by means of his own blood, thus securing an eternal redemption"* (Heb. 9:12).

Now we can sing:

There is a fountain filled with blood,
Drawn from Immanuel's veins;
And sinners, plunged beneath that flood,
Lose all their guilty stains.
(William Cowper, 1772)

CHRIST MAKING ATONEMENT

Christ made atonement for sin when He died on the cross. He was the Lamb of God without spot or blemish who substituted for sins, sin, and sinners. When Christ hung on that cruel cross, He let out seven cries. The fourth, fifth, and sixth cries have something to do with His sovereign work of atonement.

Just before His fourth cry, the whole sky took on a foreboding darkness. This darkness lasted from the sixth to the ninth hour. Then Christ gave a blood-curdling cry. *"And about the ninth hour Jesus cried out with a loud voice, saying, 'Eli, Eli, lema sabachthani?' that is, 'My God, my God, why have you forsaken me?'"* (Matt. 27:46). At that moment He was bearing spiritually the sins of men. He was dying spiritually as a sinner's substitute. Ha was bearing the sins of millions and millions and millions of people. All the believers in the Old Testament, all the believers in the New Testament, and all who would ever believe on Christ were dying in Christ that day. Christ was substituting for sinners. He bore their sins, their guilt, their penalty, their curse, and their hell! God the Father and God the Holy Spirit turned their back on God the Son as He hung there as the perfect human sacrifice for sin and sinners.

Later, Christ, knowing that He was accomplishing the salvation of sinners, uttered his fifth cry from the cross, "I thirst" (John 19:28). He was thirsty not only physically, because He was suffering the horrible physical torment and agony of a crucifixion, but also spiritually, because He was bearing the sins and torments of the damned. The fires of hell's judgment were raging inside His sinless body.

The sixth cry Christ made from the Cross was, "It is finished" (John 19:30). At that moment, Christ had accomplished atonement. His perfect and complete sacrifice for sin and sinners had been done. Salvation was forever secure for any and all sinners who would believe on the Lord Jesus Christ.

THE ESSENCE OF ATONEMENT

At the base of atonement is substitution. When the Bible says that Christ died for sin or sinners, it means that Christ died in place of, or instead of, sin and sinners. *"For our sake he made him to be sin who knew no sin, so that in him we might become the righteousness of God"* (2 Cor. 5:21). *"Christ redeemed us from the curse of the law by becoming a curse for us"* (Gal. 3:13*). "He himself bore our sins in his body on the tree, that we might die to sin and live to righteousness"* (1 Pet. 2:24). *"For even the Son of Man came not to be served but to serve, and to give his life as a ransom for many"* (Mark 10:45). Theologically, this is called *vicarious atonement.*

Since Christ died in the sinner's place, Christ bore the sinner's sins, curse, guilt, penalty, judgment, and hell. Whatever else we may say about the atonement, it is a substitution.

The atonement is not a ransom paid to Satan, nor is it the death of a martyr, nor is it a revelation of God's love, nor is it merely an example of the way of faith and obedience. All these explanations have been given by liberals in an attempt to avoid the truth of the atonement. The atonement (the death of Christ) is a penal satisfaction by substitution.

THE OBJECTS OF ATONEMENT

SINS

"Christ died for our sins ..." (1 Cor. 15:3). Christ substituted for the sins of men. *"Christ, having been offered once to bear the sins of many, will appear a second time, not to deal with sin but to save those who are eagerly waiting for him"* (Heb. 9:28). Jesus Christ died for every act of sin ever done, past, present, or future, for those who believe in Him. He made a perfect and complete substitution for sins.

Sin

"We know that our old self was crucified with him in order that the body of sin might be brought to nothing, so that we would no longer be enslaved to sin" (Rom. 6:6). At the cross, Christ, who is related by faith to the believer, judged the believer's sin nature and broke its reigning power. So now the sin nature does not have to be the Christian's master.

Sinners

"But God shows his love for us in that while we were still sinners, Christ died for us" (Rom. 5:8). *"He who did not spare his own Son but gave him up for us all, how will he not also with him graciously give us all things?"* (Rom. 8:32). Jesus Christ substituted not only for acts of sin and for the sin nature, but also for the sinner himself. He died in the place of persons. He substituted for individuals. When Christ died, He had people in mind, not merely principles. He died to save a sinful people. *"She will bear a son, and you shall call his name Jesus, for he will save his people from their sins"* (Matt. 1:21).

What can wash away my sin? Nothing but the blood of Jesus.
What can make me whole again? Nothing but the blood of Jesus.
Nothing can for sin atone. Nothing but the blood of Jesus.
Naught of good that I have done. Nothing but the blood of Jesus.
(Robert Lowry, 1876)

CONCLUSION

What then can we conclude about the atonement? The death of Christ is indispensable and absolutely necessary for human salvation. *"Indeed, under the law almost everything is purified with blood, and without the shedding of blood there is no forgiveness of sins"* (Heb. 9:22). A person can be saved only as he is covered by the blood of Christ and Christ has been substituted for him. This message of atonement and forgiveness is to be preached to the whole world.

[He] said to them, "Thus it is written, that the Christ should suffer and on the third day rise from the dead, and that repentance and forgiveness of sins should be proclaimed in his name to all nations, beginning from Jerusalem." (Luke 24:46-47).

Only when the sinner believes in Christ in simple faith and receives Him as his personal Lord and Savior, trusting wholly in Him to forgive him for his sins, can he rest assured that Christ bore his sins, penalty, guilt, curse, judgment, and hell. The church cannot forgive sins, water baptism cannot remove sins, good works cannot take away sins. Jesus Christ alone can atone for sins.

QUESTIONS:

1. From what you have learned from this chapter and from your study of the Bible, how would you define the word "atonement"?
2. How does the Old Testament prepare God's people to understand the substitutionary death of Jesus Christ?
3. Why do you need a substitute to atone for your sins? Why can't you do this for yourself? How much can you do yourself?
4. How would you explain to someone else how Christ's atoning death was for *sins*, for *sin*, and for *sinners*? Write this out and make a plan to meet with someone this very week to share this explanation.

chapter 7:

substitution

OBJECTIVES

- To know the meaning of substitution as the Bible would define it.
- To understand and believe what the Bible says about the extent of the atonement—to know for whom Christ served as a substitute.
- To understand the personal nature of salvation for us as people in union with Christ.
- To be able to respond to objections that people raise to the biblical picture of limited substitutionary atonement.

My earliest exposure to Christianity was in a free-will context. I earnestly believed that God the Father loved all men *indiscriminately*, that God the Son died for all men *inclusively*, and that God the Holy Spirit was trying to save all men *equally*. But I also believed that the three members of the Trinity could not save anyone unless a person believed what God had already done for him. I sincerely held that God had given everyone enough grace to receive Christ by his own free will and that Christ had died for every single son and daughter of Adam to make this possible. These convictions were dear to me, and I was committed to them.

In my second year of seminary, I was doing street evangelism. I walked up to a guy who was about six foot six and 260 pounds, and began to witness to him. I said to him, "Brother, do you know that God loves you and has a wonderful plan for your life?" I went on to explain to him how Christ had died for every sin he had ever committed and that God would save him if he would only believe in Jesus Christ. I did not know it then, but this man probably had some theological training in liberal Christian schools. I will never forget his reply. He said, "Does God love me the same way He loves you?" I answered, "Yes," and quoted John 3:16: *"For God so loved the world, that he gave his only Son, that whoever believes in him should not perish but have eternal life."* He then said, "Did Christ die for every sin that I have done or will do in the same way that He died for your sins?" I replied, "Absolutely." He then said, "Did Christ die for my curse, judgment, hell, and unbelief?" I again confidently replied, "Of course." He then said, "If God loves me like He loves you and Christ bore my sins, curse, judgment, and hell in the same way he bore yours, then I am saved whether I believe it or not because you told me He died for my sin of unbelief!" He then said, "Furthermore, I am not your brother. So get out of my way before I put my fist between your teeth!"

The man's reasoning left me more stunned than his actions, and for the first time I realized there might be something faulty in my understanding of God's love and Christ's death for sin. After that encounter, it took me about ten years to get my theology ironed out and to realize that the atonement was a *substitution*.

THE DEFINITION OF SUBSTITUTION

When we say "Christ died for our sins" (1 Cor. 15:3), we mean that he substituted for our sins. Christ not only died for sins but substituted for sinners. *"But God shows his love for us in that while we were still sinners, Christ died for us"* (Rom. 5:8). The Greek prepositions are *huper* and *anti*, which can mean "in place of." Substitution means that Christ died "in behalf of," "in the place of," and "in the stead of" sins and sinners.

The Bible indicates that the death of Christ is a penal satisfaction by substitution. *"For even the Son of Man came not to be served but to serve, and to give his life as a ransom for [anti] many'"* (Mark 10:45). *"He who did not spare his own Son but gave him up for us all, how will he not also with him graciously give us all things?"* (Rom. 8:32).

THE EXTENT OF SUBSTITUTION

THE ISSUE

The issue among Bible scholars is, "For whom did Christ die?" Did He die for the whole world indiscriminately or did He die for a definite number of people? Or perhaps we can ask the question, "Why did Christ die?" Did Christ die for the purpose of saving His elect seed personally and definitely? This is sometimes called the issue of limited or unlimited atonement. The issue deals with the extent of the atonement. Did Christ die for the whole world but His death is only applied to those who believe (the elect), or did He die for His elect exclusively? Did Christ die only to make the salvation of all men possible, or did He actually save men in His death? Does Christ's death merely put all men in a savable position, or does His death actually guarantee the salvation of the elect? Does Christ's death save, or does it only make a provision for all men to be saved? One view holds a limited atonement and the other a limited application of the atonement.

Let me try to explain the substitutionary death of Christ another way. Did Christ die as much for Judas as for the Apostle John? Did He substitute for Esau as well as for Jacob? When Christ hung on the cross, was He dying for a people already in hell as well as for all saints of all time? For whom did Christ propitiate the wrath of God? Who did He redeem from the curse of the Law? Who was reconciled to God? Was it all men in general or some men in particular?

John Murray, author of *Redemption Accomplished and Applied*, said,

> The question is: on whose behalf did Christ offer himself a sacrifice? On whose behalf did He propitiate the wrath of God? Whom did He reconcile to God in the body of His flesh through death? Whom did He redeem from the curse of the Law, from the guilt and power of sin, from the enthralling power and bondage of Satan? In whose stead and on whose behalf was He obedient unto death, even the death of the cross? These are precisely the questions that have to be asked and frankly faced if the matter of the extent of the atonement is to be placed in proper focus.

THE ATTITUDE

The purpose of this chapter is to prove the Bible teaches a *definite atonement*, or as it is sometimes called theologically, *particular redemption* or *limited atonement*. Before we begin this study, I confess that I do not have the last word on this subject. I also realize that there have been many godly men who believed that Christ died for the whole world indiscriminately: John Wesley, Richard Baxter, J. C. Ryle, G. Campbell Morgan, and others. Today most evangelicals hold to an unlimited atonement, including Billy Graham. The extent of the atonement is one of the most difficult subjects in the Bible, and the man who would say there are no problems with limited or unlimited atonement merely shows the shallowness of his thinking. I hold to a definite atonement because, in my opinion, it fits all the Scriptures best, has the fewest theological problems, and is logically the most consistent position.

The issue is not nearly as serious as that of free grace salvation versus free will salvation. Many servants of God accept sovereign election but also believe in unlimited atonement. This position may not be logical and consistent, but these dear brethren hold this position because they are convinced the Bible teaches an unlimited atonement. Let us each diligently search the Scriptures to see whether these things are so.

Why is it so important to wrestle with the extent of the atonement? Why is it so necessary to believe in a definite atonement? What difference could it possibly make?

First, the extent of the atonement is a biblical subject, and therefore, we should have an earnest desire to know the truth.

Second, definite atonement is important to a right preaching of the whole counsel of God. The Gospel in its most simple form is, "Christ died for our sins, and all who accept Him shall be saved." Many are truly saved who do not know, understand, or believe in particular redemption. However, a right understanding of limited atonement gives us a mature and full Gospel. Quite often a simple Gospel becomes a defective Gospel and a defective Gospel becomes a perverted Gospel. Therefore, right preaching of the Gospel is tied up with a definite atonement, for what one believes about the atonement affects how he preaches the Gospel and the methods he uses in evangelism.

Third, definite atonement is the only logical antidote to the liberal view of universalism (all men will ultimately be saved). A liberal believes that Christ died for the whole world. He bore the sin, curse, judgment, and hell of all men indiscriminately and all will ultimately be saved. This is a logical position, and liberals believe that Christ's death is effective for all men whether they believe it or not.

Fourth, definite atonement heads off the teaching of many evangelicals that Christ died for everyone in general, being very close to a universalist position. Evangelical Christians who hold to universal redemption do not believe all men will be saved. They would emphatically deny this, but their position opens the door for universalism. All the emphasis today by evangelicals to do away with hell or redefine it can be traced to their view of whether God loves all people and Christ died for all. If there was ever an hour in the history of the church when any and every form of universalism should be squelched, this is the hour!

WHAT LIMITED SUBSTITUTION DOES NOT TEACH

DEFINITE ATONEMENT DOES NOT LIMIT THE SUFFICIENCY OF THE ATONEMENT

The death of Christ has infinite, intrinsic value and is sufficient to save any and all men who will lay hold of it by faith. While Christ's death is designed to save only the elect, it is sufficient for this world and a thousand worlds just like it. Had there been ten thousand worlds with ten trillion people upon them, and had it been Christ's purpose to save all these people, Christ would have had to do no more than He did on the cross to save men. No man will ever perish for the insufficiency of the atonement to save him. If he wants this atonement, he can have it.

Definite Atonement Does Not Limit a Sincere Offer of the Gospel

The Gospel of Christ is to be offered to all men without exception, and all who want to be saved by Christ shall be saved. The atonement is objectively available to all men on the condition of faith. There is unlimited availability to all men who want the atonement.

Definite Atonement Does Not Limit Non-Saving Benefits to the World

Definite atonement does not deny the benefits that accrue to unsaved men because of the atonement, but these are non-saving benefits. Every good and profitable thing done for men is made possible by the redemptive work of Jesus Christ.

THEOLOGICAL ARGUMENTS FOR LIMITED SUBSTITUTION

Theological Statement

Negatively, the doctrine of definite atonement states that Christ was not a sacrificial substitute for every member of the human race. Positively, the doctrine of definite atonement teaches that Christ was the sacrificial substitute for a great host of sinners whom the Father had purposed from all eternity to save.

Covenant of Redemption

According to the Bible, Christ's death was part of an eternal covenant. *"Now may the God of peace who brought again from the dead our Lord Jesus, the great shepherd of the sheep, by the blood of the eternal covenant ..."* (Heb. 13:20). In Isaiah 42:6-7, the Father is speaking about the Son and says that Christ was appointed to a covenant relationship with God's people:

> *"I am the LORD; I have called you in righteousness; I will take you by the hand and keep you; I will give you as a covenant for the people, a light for the nations, to open the eyes that are blind, to bring out the prisoners from the dungeon, from the prison those who sit in darkness."*

These verses give us a hint that God the Father and God the Son covenanted together in the eternal councils to choose and redeem a people for God's glory. When Christ came to this earth, He was committed to do the Father's will. *"I can do nothing on my own. As I hear, I judge, and my judgment is just, because I seek not my own will but the will of him who sent me"* (John 5:30).

Christ made it clear that the Father's will was to save all those the Father had given Him from eternity past:

> *"All that the Father gives me will come to me, and whoever comes to me I will never cast out. For I have come down from heaven, not to do my own will but the will of him who sent me. And this is the will of him who sent me, that I should lose nothing of all that he has given me, but raise it up on the last day. For this is the will of my Father, that everyone who looks on the Son and believes in him should have eternal life, and I will raise him up on the last day." (John 6:37-40)*

In His high priestly prayer, Christ indicated that He carried out the Father's plan in redeeming God's people:

> *When Jesus had spoken these words, he lifted up his eyes to heaven, and said, "Father, the hour has come; glorify your Son that the Son may glorify you, since you have given him authority over all flesh, to give eternal life to all whom you have given him. And this is eternal life, that they know you the only true God, and Jesus Christ whom you have sent. I glorified you on earth, having accomplished the work that you gave me to do." (John 17:1-4)*

Christ prayed for the salvation, preservation, and glorification of all God's people. Who are God's people? All who trust in Jesus Christ as personal Lord and Savior.

UNION OF CHRIST WITH HIS PEOPLE

Christ has a special relationship to His people because of His union with them. God's people are "in Christ." This union took place in eternity past. *"Even as he chose us in him before the foundation of the world, that we should be holy and blameless before him"* (Eph. 1:4). This union was evident at the cross so that when Christ died, the believing sinner died. *"I have been crucified with Christ. It is no longer I who live, but Christ who lives in me. And the life I now live in the flesh I live by faith in the Son of God, who loved me and gave himself for me"* (Gal. 2:20). When Christ died, He knew every person intimately for whom He was dying. He died for the believing sinner even when He knew how horrible that sinner would be before and after conversion. Christians were in union with Christ when He died. Were unbelievers in union with Christ when He died? I think not! Furthermore, we are told that all for whom Christ died actually died in Christ, and all who died in Christ also rose with Him and share the resurrected life of Christ.

> *Do you not know that all of us who have been baptized into Christ Jesus were baptized into his death? We were buried therefore with him by baptism into death, in order that, just as Christ was raised from the dead by the glory of the Father, we too might walk in newness of life. (Rom. 6:3-4)*

We know that the unsaved do not share the life of Christ. They could not, for Christ never died for the sins of those who would not believe.

CHRIST'S WORK AS A PRIEST

The Bible teaches that Christ is the Christian's Great High Priest. Christ not only made a sacrifice of Himself for His people, but He always prays for those for whom He made this sacrifice. It is impossible to separate the atoning work of Christ from His intercession on behalf of those for whom He atoned.

> *Therefore I will divide him a portion with the many, and he shall divide the spoil with the strong, because he poured out his soul to death and was numbered with the transgressors; yet he bore the sin of many, and makes intercession for the transgressors. (Isa. 53:12)*

> *He who did not spare his own Son but gave him up for us all, how will he not also with him graciously give us all things? Who shall bring any charge against God's elect? It is God who justifies. Who is to condemn? Christ Jesus is the one who died—more than that, who was raised—who is at the right hand of God, who indeed is interceding for us. (Rom. 8:32-34)*

> *Consequently, he is able to save to the uttermost those who draw near to God through him, since he always lives to make intercession for them. (Heb. 7:25)*

Christ makes sacrifice and intercession for the same people. Does Christ pray for the world? No, the Bible says Christ does not pray for the non-elect. *"I am praying for them. I am not praying for the world but for those whom you have given me, for they are yours"* (John 17:9).

RELATIONSHIP OF CHRIST'S DEATH TO FAITH

Faith is a gift from God. *"For it has been granted to you that for the sake of Christ you should not only believe in him but also suffer for his sake"* (Phil. 1:29). *"When he arrived, he greatly helped those who through grace had believed"* (Acts 18:27b). Christ procured faith for all true believers in Christ. Christians believe because Christ purchased their faith at the cross.

> *But with the precious blood of Christ, like that of a lamb without blemish or spot. He was foreknown before the foundation of the world but was made manifest in the last times for your sake, who through him are believers in God, who raised him from the dead and gave him glory, so that your faith and hope are in God. (1 Peter 1:19-21)*

Did Christ purchase faith for everyone? No, or everyone would believe in Christ. He purchased faith for His people.

CHRIST'S FULFILLED PURPOSE

The Bible teaches that Christ came to save sinners. *"The saying is trustworthy and deserving of full acceptance, that Christ Jesus came into the world to save sinners, of whom I am the foremost"* (1 Tim. 1:15). He came to seek and to save the lost. *"'For the Son of Man came to seek and to save the lost'"* (Luke 19:10). He also came to save a people. *"She will bear a son, and you shall call his name Jesus, for he will save his people from their sins"* (Matt. 1:21). These verses do not say that His purpose was to *attempt to save* lost sinners, but *to save them*. The Scriptures tell us that Christ accomplished this purpose. *"Christ redeemed us from the curse of the law"* (Gal. 3:13); *"And you, who once were alienated and hostile in mind, doing evil deeds, he has now reconciled in his body of flesh by his death . . . ."* (Col. 1:21-22a); and *"For by a single offering he has perfected for all time those who are being sanctified"* (Heb. 10:14). These verses do not talk about a *possibility* of salvation but a *reality* of salvation.

THE DECLARATIONS OF SCRIPTURE

The Bible makes many statements to indicate that the death of Christ is limited in effect to those who believe, the elect of God. Christ said, *"Just as the Father knows me and I know the Father; and I lay down my life for the sheep"* (John 10:15), and, *"For this is my blood of the covenant, which is poured out for many for the forgiveness of sins"* (Matt. 26:28). The angel said of Jesus, *"'She will bear a son, and you shall call his name Jesus, for he will save his people from their sins'"* (Matt. 1:21). Isaiah the prophet said of Christ, *"By his knowledge shall the righteous one, my servant, make many to be accounted righteous, and he shall bear their iniquities"* (Isa. 53:11). The Apostle Paul declared, *"Christ loved the church and gave himself up for her"* (Eph. 5:25), and spoke of *"the church of God, which he obtained with his own blood"* (Acts 20:28). Further, Paul said, *"While we were still sinners, Christ died for us"* (Rom. 5:8), and Christ *"gave Himself for us"* (Titus 2:14). Paul makes it even more personal in saying, *"And the life I now live in the flesh I live by faith in the Son of God, who loved me and gave himself for me"* (Gal. 2:20). The author of Hebrews said, *"So Christ, having been offered once to bear the sins of many, will appear a second time, not to deal with sin but to save those who are eagerly waiting for him"* (Heb. 9:28). It is important to remember that all difficult passages in Scripture are to be interpreted by the clear passages.

These verses tell us that substitution for sins is found only in Christ. Men must come to Christ and Christ alone if they are to have their sins forgiven and realize that Christ bore their sin, curse, judgment, and hell.

THEOLOGICAL PROBLEM

For to this end we toil and strive, because we have our hope set on the living God, who is the Savior of all people, especially of those who believe. (1 Tim. 4:10)

UNLIMITED ATONEMENT

Christ is the Savior of all men in general, but particular to people who believe in Christ. He is a potential Savior for all, but an actual Savior for those who believe.

LIMITED ATONEMENT

The term "living God" is a reference to God the Father and not the Son. In both the Old and New Testaments the title "living God" refers to the Father. Therefore, "Savior" refers to God the Father and has nothing to do with Christ or His atonement for sin. "Savior" (1 Tim. 4:10) and "save" (1 Tim. 4:16) come from the same root and can be translated "deliverer" (deliver) or "preserver" (preserve).

The context of 1 Timothy 4 is about being saved (preserved, delivered) from the teachings of those possessed or influenced by demons: *"Now the Spirit expressly says that in later times some will depart from the faith by devoting themselves to deceitful spirits and teachings of demons, through the insincerity of liars whose consciences are seared, who forbid marriage and require abstinence from foods that God created to be received with thanksgiving by those who believe and know the truth"* (4:1-3). In verse 16, the word "save" definitely refers to physical deliverance or preservation: *"Keep a close watch on yourself and on the teaching. Persist in this, for by so doing you will save both yourself and your hearers."* Verse 16 does not refer to spiritual salvation, because this would teach a works salvation. Furthermore, the context is about deliverance from demon-influenced teachers.

Timothy was to deliver or preserve himself from demon-influenced men by keeping *"a close watch on yourself and on the teaching."*

In view of the context, why not take "Savior of all men" to mean *providential preserver of all men*, especially those who are true believers (the elect)?

This verse does not teach that Christ is the *potential* Savior of all mankind, but that He *"is* the Savior of all men." Unlimited atonement carried to its logical conclusion would teach universalism, for if Christ is the Savior of all men, then ultimately all men will be saved whether they believe or not. This is precisely the theological position of modern neo-orthodoxy.

CONCLUSION

Christ has made complete and perfect atonement for sin and sinners. His death is designed to save all who will trust in Christ. Christ's death is available to all, and all who receive Christ shall know that Christ substituted for them.

However, do not be deceived into thinking that Christ died for the sins of the whole world. He did not die in a substitutionary sense for the entire world. Christ only bore the sins of those who believe in Him. There is no substitution apart from Christ. Christ substituted for the sin, the penalty, the guilt, the curse, the condemnation, the judgment, and the hell of all who believe. The unbeliever cannot rest in some false security that because Christ died for the whole world, He must have died for him and will one day accept him into heaven. No, He substituted for God's elect people, and the elect people are those who receive Jesus Christ by faith.

The doctrine of particular redemption personalizes our salvation. When Jesus came to earth to save sinners, he had me personally on His mind. When he was hanging on the cross, taking away my sins, he had me on His mind. Christ did not just make salvation possible for me, but He actually accomplished it for me. There is nothing I can do to merit salvation because He has done it all. That is grace!

QUESTIONS:

1. From what you have learned from this chapter and from your study of the Bible, how would you define "substitution" as used in regard to salvation?
2. Where in the Bible would you find passages about the extent of the atonement?
3. Write out in your own words what it says in passages from at least three books of the Bible.
4. What is union with Christ, and how does this make Christ's substitutionary death personal for your salvation?
5. Write an outline of what you would say to answer the question "For whom did Christ die?" in response to people who would say that Christ died for all. Look for an opportunity to share it this week.

chapter 8:
redemption

OBJECTIVES

- To know the biblical meaning of the word "redemption."
- To grasp the importance of redemption along with our inability to redeem ourselves.
- To know what changes should result in our lives as we become redeemed people of God.
- To be able to respond to objections to the biblical picture that only the elect are redeemed.

A quick look at the world about us, and we see men and women who are slaves to sin. They are in bondage to habits, attitudes, and appetites. Most people do not even *want* to break the power of sin over them. But those who do have good intentions to stop certain practices often cannot. The alcoholic says he can quit whenever he wants, but rarely is successful. The adulterer and fornicator loves to fulfill his sex drives, and the person obsessed with materialism seeks only to have more. Why? Because men are captives to their passions.

Men are slaves to sin, whether done openly or in secret. Men not only are slaves to sin, but stand guilty before a holy God. A just God will punish men for their sins, great and small. Sinful men need to be delivered from this hopeless and helpless condition, and this is what redemption is all about -God delivering slaves from sin and making them free in Christ.

DEFINITION OF REDEMPTION

The Greek New Testament uses four words to explain redemption: *agorazo*, which means "to purchase, buy, or redeem"; *exagorazo*, which means "to purchase out"; *lutrosis*, which means "to purchase by the paying of a ransom price"; and *apolutrosis*, which means "to purchase by the paying of a ransom and to set free."

From these four Greek words, all translated "redeem" or "redemption" in the English Bible, we can form a complete definition: redemption means to purchase out of sin and set free by the paying of a ransom price. Redemption implies not only purchase out of sin but also release from sin.

NEED FOR REDEMPTION

Men need to be redeemed because they are sinners. They are not only guilty of acts of sin, but actually slaves to sin. Jesus Christ taught that men are slaves to sin because they are by nature sinners. *"Jesus answered them, 'Truly, truly, I say to you, everyone who commits sin is a slave to sin'"* (John 8:34). Before conversion to Christ, a man is engulfed and dominated by his sinful passions. The unsaved man may or may not commit gross, immoral acts of sin, but he always loves for himself and not for God. The non-Christian loves to please himself. Money may become the all-consuming goal of his life; pleasure may occupy his every thought; status among men may be the constant pursuit of his being. Man without Christ is captive to habits, attitudes, and appetites, and his whole life is designed to further the "Big I."

Men are servants of sin because they willingly present themselves to sin. Unsaved men are the moral subjects of their sinful natures. They are hopeless and helpless slaves to sin and they stand under the judgment of God. They must face punishment for their sins before a holy and righteous God. All men outside Christ are in desperate need of being freed from this terrible bondage to sin. Without redemption, man shall perish in his sins. *"I told you that you would die in your sins, for unless you believe that I am he you will die in your sins"* (John 8:24).

PICTURE OF REDEMPTION IN THE OLD TESTAMENT

Redemption cannot be understood properly without a good grasp of the meaning of redemption in the Old Testament. The New Testament builds on the Old Testament, and this is no more evident than when it deals with the concept of redemption.

The Old Testament often speaks about Israel as a purchased people. *"Terror and dread fall upon them [enemies of Israel]; because of the greatness of your arm, they are still as a stone, till your people, O LORD, pass by, till the people pass by whom you have purchased"* Ex. 15:16), or as *"The Holy People, The Redeemed of the LORD"* (Is 62:12). True Israel was redeemed of God, and that redemption was portrayed in the Passover feast (Ex. 12). The nation had been slaves to Egypt for over four hundred years. They were under the yoke of cruel Egyptian taskmasters. God sent His servant Moses to lead the people out of Egypt into the Promised Land. God brought nine plagues on Egypt, but Pharaoh would not let the people go. God then brought the tenth plague, the death of the firstborn of every family in Egypt.

Israel could avoid this plague only by carefully observing the Passover. Each Jewish household was to slay a lamb and put the blood on the two doorposts and lintel so the death angel would pass over Jewish homes. *"The blood shall be a sign for you, on the houses where you are. And when I see the blood, I will pass over you, and no plague will befall you to destroy you, when I strike the land of Egypt"* (Ex. 12:13). The blood protected the Jews from the judgment of the plague and gave them the basis for leaving Egypt. Those who were blood - covered were purchased out of slavery in Egypt. They were a redeemed people in a temporal sense, bought out of slavery with the blood.

FACT OF REDEMPTION IN THE NEW TESTAMENT

Redemption finds its fulfillment in Christ, who purchased His people out of their sins. *"[They] are justified by his grace as a gift, through the redemption that is in Christ Jesus"* (Rom. 3:24). *"In him we have redemption through his blood, the forgiveness of our trespasses, according to the riches of his grace"* (Eph. 1:7). Christians are said to be redeemed by Christ.

Redemption is often connected with the Athenian marketplace called the Agora, where many things were sold, most notably slaves. Almost half the Roman and Greek populations were slaves to the other half. This was without regard to color or race. Slave traders would purchase these bond slaves by paying a handsome price for them. They would be purchased out of the market of slavery and become the bond slave of their new masters.

This is a vivid picture of the unsaved man, who is a slave to sin and in bondage to the slave market of sin because of his own sinful nature. God, through the paying of the ransom price of Christ's death, purchased the sinner out of the slave market of sin. Yet from the Greek word *apolutrosis*, we know that He not only purchases us out of slavery, but sets us free forever from the guilt, penalty, and bondage of sin.

Martin Luther, before his conversion to Christ, was a Roman Catholic priest. He knew he was a sinner and under the curse of the law. He felt himself a slave to sin and did not know how to find release. He trusted Christ to save him and obtained glorious release from the guilt and penalty of sin. He began a life of being progressively set free in Christ. Luther renamed himself "Martin Eleutheros," which in Greek means "Martin the free." Christ set Luther free!

The New Testament clearly tells us that the means of redemption is the blood of Jesus Christ. *"Knowing that you were ransomed from the futile ways inherited from your forefathers, not with perishable things such as silver or gold, but with the precious blood of Christ, like that of a lamb without blemish or spot"* (1 Peter 1:18-19). Christ's blood was shed to purchase His church. *"Pay careful attention to yourselves and to all the flock, in which the Holy Spirit has made you overseers, to care for the church of God, which he obtained with his own blood"* (Acts 20:28). The blood of Christ not only saves, but it saves a multitude that no man can number.

"And they sang a new song, saying, 'Worthy are you to take the scroll and to open its seals, for you were slain, and by your blood you ransomed people for God from every tribe and language and people and nation'" (Rev. 5:9). It is because Christ shed His precious blood that He has purchased an eternal redemption for us. *"He entered once for all into the holy places, not by means of the blood of goats and calves but by means of his own blood, thus securing an eternal redemption"* (Heb. 9:12). The shedding of Christ's blood speaks of His substitutionary sacrifice for sins. He paid the ransom for sinners. He made the payment for sin in the sinner's place. *"Even as the Son of Man came not to be served but to serve, and to give his life as a ransom for many"* (Matt. 20:28).

OBJECTS OF REDEMPTION

When Christ died on the cross, He paid the ransom price for sin and sinners. His blood purchased sinful men out of the slave market of sin. *"In whom [Christ] we have redemption, the forgiveness of sins"* (Col. 1:14). We were not able to pay the price but, thank God, Christ has come and paid the price for us. The Lord Jesus Christ came to ransom us, to deliver us. He has paid the price, and so the prison in which we were held captive by sin and the devil has been opened, and we who were slaves have been made free.

Suppose I was given a traffic ticket. I was guilty before the law and in debt to the law. When I appear in court, the judge listens patiently to my story and even may be somewhat sympathetic. But I have broken the law and must pay the penalty. The judge passes a just sentence of fifteen days in jail or $500 fine. I have no cash, no way to pay the fine. Therefore, I must spend fifteen days in jail - the just penalty for breaking the law. Just when I am about at the point of despair, the judge says, "Mr. Arnold, out of the good pleasure of my own will, I am going to pay this debt of $500 for you." He lays out the money and says, "You may go free now, Mr. Arnold." All I can do is thank him for his graciousness and leave a free man. The judge passed a just sentence on me and then paid the debt for me. Being a free man, I would be indebted to that judge and would probably do anything for him.

Another aspect of redemption is the Christian's body. The redemption Christ made for us became effective the instant we believed in Christ. He purchased our whole salvation, body and soul, and we were positionally redeemed and our redemption was certain. Experientially, however, we still sin, but one day we shall receive a total, complete redemption when we receive our resurrected bodies. *"And not only the creation, but we ourselves, who have the firstfruits of the Spirit, groan inwardly as we wait eagerly for adoption as sons, the redemption of our bodies"* (Rom. 8:23). Every Christian is waiting for his redeemed body, which will be free from the presence of sin forever:

In him you also ... were sealed with the promised Holy Spirit, who is the guarantee of our inheritance until we acquire possession of it, to the praise of his glory. (Eph. 1:13-14)

And do not grieve the Holy Spirit of God, by whom you were sealed for the day of redemption. (Eph. 4:30)

RESULTS OF REDEMPTION

REDEEMED FROM SIN

[Christ] gave himself for us to redeem us from all lawlessness and to purify for himself a people for his own possession who are zealous for good works. (Titus 2:14)

The Christian has been redeemed from the guilt and the penalty of sin. Every lawless deed we have ever done is covered by the blood of Christ. The believer has been purchased out of the slave market of sin and has been set at liberty. Sin will not have dominion over the Christian as it did before he was saved. Since the Christian is purchased with blood, he is not to be hung up in the habits, attitudes, and appetites of the unsaved world:

Were you a slave when called? Do not be concerned about it. But if you can gain your freedom, avail yourself of the opportunity. For he who was called in the Lord as a slave is a freedman of the Lord. Likewise he who was free when called is a slave of Christ. You were bought with a price; do not become slaves of men. (1Cor. 7:21-23)

REDEEMED FROM THE LAW

Christ redeemed us from the curse of the law by becoming a curse for us—for it is written, "Cursed is everyone who is hanged on a tree." (Gal. 3:13)

The Law, namely the Ten Commandments, condemns men, for the Law shows men they are sinners and under a curse. Christ has redeemed the Christian out from under the Law and its demands; therefore, we are not under the curse.

Who [Christ] gave himself for our sins to deliver us from the present evil age, according to the will of our God and Father. (Gal. 1:4)

The Christian has been positionally purchased out of this evil age. This age is evil because it is controlled by Satan, who is the god of this age. *"And even if our Gospel is veiled, it is veiled only to those who are perishing. In their case the god of this world has blinded the minds of the unbelievers, to keep them from seeing the light of the Gospel of the glory of Christ, who is the image of God"* (2 Cor. 4:3-4). Christians are a people purchased with blood and positionally separated by God from this evil age and from this world system.

A redeemed person can flirt with the world but never return completely to the world system because Christ has redeemed him out of it. Those Christians who flirt with the world will be deeply convicted by God and disciplined until they realize they have been bought with a price and belong to the living Christ.

PURPOSE OF REDEMPTION

God had a definite purpose or design in redeeming men for Himself through the death of Christ. God's design in redemption will be accomplished, and the evidence of being a purchased child of God will come out in good works.

To Appreciate the Forgiveness of Sins

In whom [Christ] we have redemption, the forgiveness of sins. (Col. 1:14)

The Christian, because of redemption, has the forgiveness of all sins, past, present, and future. This is pure grace, and grace should make us desire to love and serve Christ even more as His redeemed children.

In the early twentieth century, some archaeologists discovered some valuable business and personal letters written in New Testament or *Koine* Greek. One of the letters was about a woman who was for sale in the slave market. Apparently she was quite attractive and would have made a fine slave for any master. A slave trader purchased this woman for a very high price. After the purchase, for no reason other than the good pleasure of his own will, he told the woman, "I have paid a high price for you and have bought you out of slavery. Now I set you free forever. You never have to be my slave or anyone's slave again." He then turned and walked away and she stood there a free woman. A few minutes later the slave trader heard footsteps pounding behind him and a weeping woman's voice crying, "Sir, Sir!" He said, "What do you want with me, woman, I have set you free forever." The woman cried out, "My Lord, for your kindness and graciousness in setting me free, I will voluntarily be your slave forever. You are now my master!" So it is for the Christian. When he comes to understand that he was a slave to sin and that Christ purchased him out from the slave market of sin, he voluntarily makes himself a slave of Christ.

TO BE A PURCHASED POSSESSION

> *But you are a chosen race, a royal priesthood, a holy nation, a people for his own possession, that you may proclaim the excellencies of him who called you out of darkness into his marvelous light. (1 Peter 2:9)*

The King James Version says Christians are a "peculiar people," and the New American Standard Version renders it "a people for God's own possession." This means literally "a purchased possession people." The Christian has been purchased by the highest price that could ever be paid for a slave in bondage to sin—the death of Jesus Christ. We Christians are a purchased people and we should live like people bought with blood.

TO LIVE HOLY LIVES

> *Or do you not know that your body is a temple of the Holy Spirit within you, whom you have from God? You are not your own, for you were bought with a price So glorify God in your body. (1 Cor. 6:19-20)*

The Christian is no longer his own master, for he has been bought with the price of Christ's blood. He belongs to another, Christ Jesus. Redemption has made it possible for the Holy Spirit to indwell the Christian. Now the Christian can live a holy life. *"Who [Christ] gave himself for us to redeem us from all lawlessness and to purify for himself a people for his own possession who are zealous for good works"* (Titus 2:14). A proper understanding of redemption gives new motivation for a life of holiness and service. If you were on trial accused of being a Christian, would there be enough evidence to convict you?

EXTENT OF REDEMPTION

> *But false prophets also arose among the people, just as there will be false teachers among you, who will secretly bring in destructive heresies, even denying the Master who bought them, bringing upon themselves swift destruction. (2 Peter 2:1)*

We are faced in 2 Peter 2:1 with the question, "Did Christ's death merely make the redemption of all men possible, or did His death actually redeem the elect seed particularly and definitely. Second Peter 2:1 is the most difficult verse to interpret for those who believe in a definite atonement or particular redemption. If it were not for this verse, limited atonement would be transparently clear to most people. This verse seems on the surface to teach that some men who are bought by the Lord Jesus shall perish and not be saved, for it says that these false teachers are *"denying the Master [despotase] who bought [agprazo] them, bringing upon themselves swift destruction."* Christian scholars who believe in unlimited or universal atonement say this verse teaches that Christ bought (*agorazo*) these false teachers but did not purchase them out (*exagorazo*) of sin because they did not believe. Admittedly, this is a difficult verse. I do have several answers that satisfy me but they may not satisfy you.

GENERAL OBSERVATIONS

FACTS ABOUT DESPOTASE (MASTER LORD)

The word *despotase* (Lord, Master) is usually used of God the Father when in a context of dominion and sovereignty. *"And when they heard it, they lifted their voices together to God and said, 'Sovereign Lord [despota], who made the heaven and the earth and the sea and everything in them'"* (Acts 4:24). *"They cried out with a loud voice, 'O Sovereign Lord [despotes], holy and true, how long before you will judge and avenge our blood on those who dwell on the earth?'"* (Rev. 6:10). When Christ is viewed in His sovereignty and dominion, the Greek word *kurios* (Lord) is almost always used.

It is a good possibility that *depostase* does not refer to Christ at all in 2 Peter 1:17 – 2:4, but to God the Father. If so, then 2 Peter 2:1 is taken out of the realm of the atonement, for it has nothing to do with the person or work of Christ.

An astute Bible student would point to Jude 4, where it seems as though Christ is referred to as *despotase: "For certain people have crept in unnoticed who long ago were designated for this condemnation, ungodly people, who pervert the grace of our God into sensuality and deny our only Master and Lord, Jesus Christ."* The context of Jude 4 is about false teachers, as is 2 Peter 2:1; therefore, *despotase* must refer to Jesus Christ. It should be pointed out, however, that the context of Jude 4 is about Christ's sovereignty and dominion over man, and not His mediatorship.

Despotase is used about thirty times in the Bible — twenty times in the Greek Old Testament (Septuagint) and ten times in the New Testament. It never refers to the Father or Son as mediator, unless 2 Peter 2:1 be an exception. If *despotase* in 2 Peter 2:1 does refer to Christ, it refers to His sovereignty and not to Him as redeemer-mediator. The argument of 2 Peter 2:1 is taken out of the realm of the atonement and placed in the person of Christ and His sovereignty.

Of its thirty uses in the New Testament, *agorazo* is never used in a soteriological (spiritual salvation) context (unless 2 Peter 2:1 be an exception) without the word for "price" (a technical term for the blood of Christ) or its equivalent being stated or made explicit in the context: *"For you were bought with a price"* (1 Cor. 6:20). *"You were bought with a price; do not become slaves of men"* (1 Cor. 7:23). *"'For you were slain, and by your blood you ransomed people for God from every tribe and language and people and nation'"* (Rev. 5:9b). When terms other than *agorazo* are used, the price is also mentioned. *"Pay careful attention to yourselves and to all the flock, in which the Holy Spirit has made you overseers, to care for the church of God, which he obtained with his own blood"* (Acts 20:28). *"In him we have redemption through his blood, the forgiveness of our trespasses, according to the riches of his grace"* (Eph. 1:7). *"Knowing that you were ransomed from the futile ways inherited from your forefathers, not with perishable things such as silver or gold, but with the precious blood of Christ, like that of a lamb without blemish or spot"* 1 Peter 1:18-19).

It could be that *agorazo* is not related to the atonement at all in 2 Peter 2:1, for nothing is said in context of Christ dying for any persons or the paying of a price.

In the five references to *agorazo* in the New Testament, the extent of the purchase is limited to believers (the elect) and is never related to non-believers.

In contexts in which no payment price is stated or implied, *agorazo* may be translated "acquire" or "obtain." No payment price is mentioned in 2 Peter 2:1 so perhaps the word *agorazo* should not be translated "to buy."

Agorazo is never used in the Bible in a hypothetical sense, unless 2 Peter 2:1 is the exception. It is always used in contexts in which the buying or acquiring takes place in reality.

WHAT 2 PETER 2:1 DOES TEACH

These facts help us to understand what 2 Peter 2:1 does not teach. It does not teach universal redemption. However, we do have a problem as to what 2 Peter 2:1 *does* teach.

VIEW # 1: PROFESSIONS OF FALSE TEACHERS *(Soteriological)*

One possible interpretation is the Christian Charity View. This position takes Christ as the mediator, and the word *agorazo* as referring to spiritual salvation. These false teachers were professing to be what in reality they were not; that is, they were claiming to be bought (redeemed) but were not because they were denying Him. They said they belonged to the Lord but they did not. Peter is just taking their own testimony at face value, but does not affirm it as true.

81

Another possible view is to see the false teachers as created by the sovereign Lord for the specific end of destruction. These false teachers ware denying the sovereign God and Christ who created them. We would then translate this verse "denying the Master who created them."

Peter is quoting from Deut. 32:5-6 where God is dealing with Israel as those who profess to be believers and members of the covenant relationship. Yet Israel was a stiff-necked people and many were not saved even though they were under the covenant of grace and called *"the people ... whom you have purchased"* (Ex. 15:16). Deut. 32:5-6 says:

> *They have dealt corruptly with him; they are no longer his children because they are blemished; they are a crooked and twisted generation. Do you thus repay the LORD, you foolish and senseless people? Is not he your father, who created you, who made you and established you?*

Deut. 32:5-6 teaches that the pre-incarnate God (Christ), the sovereign Lord, owns the covenant nation of Israel because He made and established them to be a covenant and privileged people who were to be to Him "a kingdom of priests and a holy nation" (Ex. 19:6).

Second Peter 2:12 says that these false teachers had a place in God's sovereign plan: *"But these, like irrational animals, creatures of instinct, born to be caught and destroyed, blaspheming about matters of which they are ignorant, will also be destroyed in their destruction."* Destruction was part of God's plan for false teachers.

Just as God sovereignly acquired Israel out of Egypt in order to make her a covenant nation because He had created her for that purpose, so Christ, the sovereign Lord, acquired the false teachers in order to make them a part of the covenant nation of God in the flesh because He created them within the mystery of His providence, for the purpose of bringing glory to Himself through their foreordainment unto condemnation. (Dr. Gary Long, "Paper on Second Peter 2:1")

The argument fits the context of 2 Peter 2 and the overall argument of this letter from Peter. It is consistent with other teachings on false teachers: *"For certain people have crept in unnoticed who long ago were designated for this condemnation, ungodly people, who pervert the grace of our God into sensuality and deny our only Master and Lord, Jesus Christ"* (Jude 4). It also is consistent with God's sovereign purposes for the wicked: *"What if God, desiring to show his wrath and to make known his power, has endured with much patience vessels of wrath prepared for destruction, in order to make known the riches of his glory for vessels of mercy, which he has prepared beforehand for glory—even us whom he has called, not from the Jews only but also from the Gentiles?"* (Rom. 9:22-24). Second Peter 2:1 fits nicely into the teaching of definite atonement.

CONCLUSION

The unregenerate is a slave to his own nature and passions. He needs deliverance; he needs redemption; he needs to be purchased out of the slave market of sin. He is guilty before God and under condemnation for his sin. Only Christ can deliver him from the guilt and the penalty of sin through His death on the cross for sin and sinners. Trusting Christ for redemption is the first step in being delivered from fleshly habits, attitudes, and appetites. The sinner owes a debt to God, and there is no way he can pay this debt. However, God has provided a way by which another, Jesus Christ, has already paid that debt. This debt was paid at the cross when Jesus Christ paid the price for the sins of men. For whom did Christ pay this debt? He paid it for all who believe in Jesus Christ as Lord and Savior. Christ paid the price for the Christian's salvation, and His perfect death for sin will be accredited to his account forever.

Christ not only paid the ransom price of His blood to redeem us, but will set us free so that sin will never have dominion over us again and the curse of the Law will never touch us. Then we can say, "I am Jack, the free; I am Jane, the free; I am Earl, the free; I am Betty, the free!" When Christ redeems people, He sets them free forever.

QUESTIONS:
1. From what you have learned from this chapter and from your study of the Bible, how would you define the word "redemption"?
2. What do we learn about redemption from its parallel with release from slavery?
3. What does this show us about the importance of redemption in our spiritual lives?
4. How should our lives be different as people redeemed from bondage to sin? Point to two or three biblical passages that direct our lives.
5. Write out how you would respond to the objection that 2 Peter 2:1 indicates Christ's death only made redemption possible, and not particular or specific to the elect. Look for an opportunity this week to share this explanation.

chapter 9:
forgiveness

OBJECTIVES

• To know the biblical meaning of "forgiveness."
• To understand our need for forgiveness because of the depth of our sin.
• To grasp from Scripture the desire of God and the ability and means of God to forgive sins.
• To be able and willing to forgive and be forgiven in human relationships.

Every person in this world is either in need of receiving forgiveness or in need of giving forgiveness, or both. We live in a fallen, sinful world, and the whole world is somehow spiritually dysfunctional. Whether saved or unsaved, we may be struggling with at least some of the following problems:

1. A husband and wife have been cold and indifferent, and not had intimate relations for years. Both need to give and receive forgiveness.
2. A husband has been negative, critical, and harsh toward his wife. He needs forgiveness. She needs to give forgiveness.
3. A teenage girl has been sexually abused by a father or a brother, and she is angry, depressed, and confused in her emotions. She needs to give forgiveness to the one who violated her. (This does not mean he should avoid the consequences of his crimes, though. Nor should she necessarily trust him again.)
4. A boy watches his mother leave his dad for an adulterous affair with his uncle. The mother has abandoned him. When he grows older, he is confused, angry, and bitter with his mother. The mother needs forgiveness. He needs to forgive his mother, even if she never admits to her sin. (Again, this does not mean she should necessarily be trusted again.)
5. A man or woman has fallen into a sinful sexual relationship outside marriage. The woman may be pregnant and may have had an abortion. Both partners in the sin need to receive forgiveness. (The offended party does not necessarily have to trust the guilty party or parties, however.)

6. A man or woman has given into alcohol or drug abuse and messed up his or her life, to the point of destroying relationships. He or she needs to receive forgiveness. (This does not necessarily mean that others have to trust the addict again.)
7. A person has either gossiped or been the victim of gossip. In either case, the person needs to receive or give forgiveness.

Hundreds of situations require forgiveness. Fathers are at odds with sons. Daughters are alienated from mothers. Brothers and sisters have not spoken for years. Friendships are strained because of sin, wrong perceptions, or misunderstandings. We have the negative emotions of hurt, betrayal, anger, and bitterness. How do we come to grips with the angry person within us? How can we find forgiveness and give forgiveness? Where do we get the strength to forgive? The Bible has the answers, and we must believe the Scriptures above any negative feelings. Feelings are deceptive, but the Bible is true. One of the major challenges of Christian living is to have the Bible rule our feelings rather than our feelings overrule the Bible.

DEFINITION OF FORGIVENESS

There are several Greek words for forgiveness, but the primary word is *aphiami*. It means "to dismiss, release, send away, liberate." Forgiveness means to dismiss, release, or liberate a criminal from a spiritual prison.

Another meaning of *aphiami* is "send away" or "let go." When Christ was on the cross, he said of those who put Him to death, *"'Father, forgive them, for they know not what they do'"* (Luke 23:34). Ignorance, however, is never a basis for forgiveness. It may be that Christ meant, "Father, let them go, for they do not know what they are doing." Christ asked the Father that His enemies be let go, so they would live another day to become saved. Within the concept of "forgiveness" is the idea of "letting go." This secondary definition is very important for Christians as they deal with the concept of forgiveness.

NEED FOR FORGIVENESS

All people are sinful. *"For all have sinned and fall short of the glory of God"* (Rom. 3:23). Every person in the world is in debt to God because of sin. The debt is so great that no person can ever get forgiveness for that debt and be delivered from the curse, bondage, and condemnation, apart from divine intervention. A single sin puts us in debt to a holy, righteous, perfect God. The judgment is the same for a person who steals from the cookie jar as it is for one who robs a bank. All men are in a hopeless and helpless spiritual condition. Only God can deliver, release, and set men and women, boys and girls, free from the prison of sin.

Not until we understand the depth of our sin before a holy God will we flee to Christ for forgiveness. To the degree that we understand our sinfulness, we will appreciate our salvation in Christ. This truth is seen in Christ's words about a prostitute: *"Therefore I tell you, her sins, which are many, are forgiven—for she loved much. But he who is forgiven little, loves little"* (Luke 7:47).

GOD OF FORGIVENESS

If men are so sinful, how do we know that a holy, righteous, wrathful God will forgive anyone? The Bible declares that He is a forgiving God. *" 'But you are a God ready to forgive, gracious and merciful, slow to anger and abounding in steadfast love, and did not forsake them' "* (Neh. 9:17). God is anxious and willing to forgive. *"For you, O Lord, are good and forgiving, abounding in steadfast love to all who call upon you"* (Psa. 86:5). *"The LORD is slow to anger and abounding in steadfast love, forgiving iniquity and transgression ..."* (Num. 14:18). God's eagerness to forgive sins should cause us to fear Him, to stand in awe of His greatness. *"But with you there is forgiveness, that you may be feared"* (Psa. 130:4).

Never doubt God's ability or willingness to forgive sins that you commit before becoming a Christian, or even afterward. He is by nature a forgiving God. He is not fickle or inconsistent like men. God can never go against His perfect nature.

Only God can forgive sins. *"Who can forgive sins but God alone?"* (Mark 2:7)? *" 'But that you may know that the Son of Man has authority on earth to forgive sins"—he said to the man who was paralyzed—"I say to you, rise, pick up your bed and go home' "* (Luke 5:24). No priest, pastor, or pope has power to forgive sins. Nor does a counselor. All counseling must direct people to God alone who forgives completely, totally, and perfectly for any and every sin. He is a forgiving God.

UNSAVED AND FORGIVENESS

The death of Christ is the reason that people are able to have forgiveness from God. Forgiveness can be found only in Christ. *"In him we have redemption through his blood, the forgiveness of our trespasses, according to the riches of his grace, which he lavished upon us, in all wisdom and insight"* (Eph. 1:7). The person who receives Christ by faith alone will be delivered from the slave market of sin, forgiven, and set free forever. Where is forgiveness located? It is located in the blood or death of Christ for sin. The Bible says, *"Indeed, under the law almost everything is purified with blood, and without the shedding of blood there is no forgiveness of sins"* (Heb. 9:22). Forgiveness is by God's grace alone, not according to law, works, or acts of merit. If a man or woman or boy or girl is forgiven, it is because of God's sovereign grace. You say, "But don't we have to believe and trust in Christ to be saved, and is that not something we do?" Yes, we have to believe, and we exercise that belief. *"To him all the prophets bear witness that everyone who believes in him receives forgiveness of sins through his name"* (Acts 10:43). Yet, even the act of faith is a gift from the hand of a gracious God. *"And when [Apollos] wished to cross* to Achaia, the brothers encouraged him and wrote to the disciples to welcome him. When he arrived, he greatly helped those who through grace had believed" (Acts 18:27). Faith is a gracious gift from God, but God does not exercise this faith for us. We must make a deliberate, conscious, and voluntary decision to have Christ as our Lord and Savior. When we do receive Christ, we look back and realize that even our faith comes from God, and He should have all the glory for our salvation.

For you who are not Christians, understand that there is no sin you have ever done that Christ cannot or will not forgive. No sin is more potent than Christ's blood that provides forgiveness for sins. Christ forgave a prostitute and said, *"Therefore I tell you, her sins, which are many, are forgiven—for she loved much"* (Luke 7:47). Before his conversion, the Apostle Paul was an accomplice to the murder of Christians, but he was forgiven:

> The saying is trustworthy and deserving of full acceptance, that Christ Jesus came into the world to save sinners, of whom I am the foremost. But I received mercy for this reason, that in me, as the foremost, Jesus Christ might display his perfect patience as an example to those who were to believe in him for eternal life. (1 Tim. 1:15-16)

God is a forgiving God. He longs to forgive sinful people. God not only forgives every sin ever done, but He *forgets* the sin. *"For I will be merciful toward their iniquities, and I will remember their sins no more"* (Heb. 8:12). How an all-knowing God forgets sin, we will never comprehend with our finite minds. Since he *does* forget sin, we do not have to figure it out, but we have to believe it.

My oldest son, Mark, received Christ as Savior and Lord at 16 1/2 years of age. Before this time, he was very rebellious toward Christ. The night he confessed to me he had become a Christian, he said, "Dad, are you sure God can forgive for *any* sin?" "Yes," I said, "Any sin." My mind thought, "What great sin has he done to ask that question—sex, drugs, some criminal activity?" It was 25 years later I found out the answer to Mark's question. Mark confessed to Carol and me and to the world that when he was in his early teens, he was sexually abused by his basketball coach. My answer then was the same as before, "Yes, any sin." God forgave and forgot Mark's sin, but it took 25 years for Mark to come to grips with that sin. He learned to forgive that man who offended him so terribly.

SAVED AND FORGIVENESS

Forgiveness is not only for every sin we committed before receiving Christ as Savior and Lord. As Christians, still plagued by the sin of Adam, we need forgiveness now, for the sins we continue to commit. In a legal and positional sense, Christ died for every sin that every Christian would ever do—past, present, and future. In a legal sense, there is always forgiveness for the true believer in Christ. The blood of Christ cleanses from sins already committed and sins we are committing right now. *"But if we walk in the light, as he is in the light, we have fellowship with one another, and the blood of Jesus his Son cleanses us from all sin"* (1 John 1:7).

Because of our eternal, positional forgiveness—forgiveness for no other reason than that we are in relationship with Christ—there is no condemnation for the true child of God. *"There is therefore now no condemnation for those who are in Christ Jesus"* (Rom 8:1).

For any sin a Christian does, there is forgiveness. A loving Heavenly Father must forgive the Christian based on the death of Christ. *"If we confess our sins, he is faithful and just to forgive us our sins and to cleanse us from all unrighteousness"* (1 John 1:9). God's justice demands that He be true to Himself, and God's faithfulness demands that He be true to His Word. We do not trust our feelings but, by faith, we trust God and the promises of forgiveness. Feelings will follow when faith has been exercised. While there is forgiveness for any sin the Christian commits, this does not mean God delights in our sin or wants us to sin so He can give us more cleansing. *"My little children, I am writing these things to you so that you may not sin. But if anyone does sin, we have an advocate with the Father, Jesus Christ the righteous"* (1 John 2:1). The Christian is called to keep God's moral will as expressed in the moral law. God is never pleased when His children choose to sin (and every sin we do is by choice).

Acts of sin put the Christian out of temporal fellowship with God the Father, though not out of eternal fellowship. When a Christian chooses to sin, He will receive loving discipline from the Heavenly Father. Yet, God has provided a way to receive forgiveness and experience daily communion or experiential fellowship with Christ. God's means for experiencing fellowship is confession of our sins. *"If we confess our sins, he is faithful and just to forgive us our sins and to cleanse us from all unrighteousness"* (1 John 1:9). He has promised by His justice and faithfulness to forgive us of our sins.

While the Heavenly Father will forgive any act of sin a Christian may do, there will be consequences in this world for that sin, and most likely some kind of loving discipline. Sometimes the divine discipline can be very harsh, but it is always designed to drive the Christian to repentance. God is far more concerned than we are that Christians walk a godly life. We need to fear our Heavenly Father's discipline, but never fear his eternal wrath for our sins. Christ has taken care of that at the cross. Yet, we must understand that sometimes divine discipline is merely suffering the worldly consequences for our choice to sin. If a Christian chooses to rob a bank, then he must be prepared to go to jail. If a Christian woman chooses to have a sexual affair, she can find forgiveness, but she will have to face the horrible guilt of sin, possibly become pregnant, and, even worse, murder that child through abortion. If a Christian husband chooses to be an adulterer, he can be forgiven, but he will face the guilt of unfaithfulness, and possibly lose his family through divorce. If a Christian man or woman in anger chooses to murder someone, he or she can be forgiven, but still faces life in prison or the death penalty. There are always consequences for acts of sin.

There was a young lady who was raised in a Christian home and sent to a Christian school, but in the Christian school, she began to mess around with drugs. Then her whole life became consumed with drugs, and soon she fell into sexual sin. She was raped by a man. She became pregnant by another man. This young woman asked her parents, "Why do bad things happen to good people? Why did I get raped? Why did God allow me to get pregnant?" First, she had bad theology. There are no good people, and her actions proved it. Second, she was suffering the expected consequences of making bad choices and going against the moral will of God. There are serious consequences for making choices that violate God's moral law. What this woman really needed was forgiveness, but sin had so hardened her heart that she thought she was a good person, and that God should somehow reward her for bad choices. She needed forgiveness on God's terms, not hers.

RELATIONSHIPS AND FORGIVENESS

Forgiveness is a major factor in relationships, as Jesus says over and over again. *"For if you forgive others their trespasses, your heavenly Father will also forgive you, but if you do not forgive others their trespasses, neither will your Father forgive your trespasses"* (Matt. 6:14-15). *"Judge not, and you will not be judged; condemn not, and you will not be condemned; forgive, and you will be forgiven"* (Luke 6:37). This is not a reference to eternal forgiveness but to the experience of forgiveness in time. Christians are to forgive those who sin against them, offend them, hurt them, disappoint them. Even their enemies are to be loved and forgiven. It is impossible to forgive our enemies in our own strength, but by the power of Christ at work in us, we can forgive.

In a former pastorate my church hired a great man to become my associate. Soon after his coming, I fell into a deep depression and was emotionally disturbed. I became very strained with the new associate. During this time, ugly things were said about me. A few were true, but most were allegations that had no support. There were perceptions, lies, and rumors about me. I became distrustful, angry and bitter. I was disillusioned with Christians and the local church. My expectations, obviously, were too high for Christian leaders and lay people. The result of all this was a church split, and I ended up leaving the church two years later. The damage was horrific – bad relationship with my associate, distrust of my elders, frustration with the congregation. I was eaten up with bitterness. I needed forgiveness from God, and I needed to give forgiveness to others. I left the church and found forgiveness from God, but I needed to ask for forgiveness from those I offended, whether they gave it to me or not. A year later, I righted things with the elders and people, asking for their forgiveness for any actions that were displeasing to God and offensive to them. They forgave me. Ten years later, God put on my heart to go to my estranged former associate, and ask for forgiveness for anything I did to offend him. We met in a public restaurant. I asked for his forgiveness, and he asked for mine. Right in the middle of the restaurant, we hugged and cried. God restored a relationship by giving forgiveness. We were brothers in Christ who had been forgiven by Christ, and now we could forgive one another. Today this pastor is one of my closest friends in the ministry. The God of forgiveness does miracles! We are commanded to forgive brothers and sisters in Christ. *"Be kind to one another, tenderhearted, forgiving one another, as God in Christ forgave you"* (Eph. 4:32). How can we forgive Christians who have deeply hurt us, broken our trust, and wounded our consciences? We can forgive only as we relate our hurt, anger, disappointment, and bitterness back to the cross of Christ, where He died for our sins and the sins of those who trespass against us. *". . . forgiving one another, as God in Christ forgave you"* (Eph. 4:32b).

We must remember there are no perfect people. Every Christian at some time or another will not meet our expectations, or will say or do something that wounds our hearts. Our mates, our children, our pastors, our elders, our closest friends, and our Christian idols will disappoint or even betray us. We must learn to forgive, or we will end up bitter people who do nothing but judge and criticize.

How many times must we forgive those who offend us? The Bible says, *"Then Peter came up and said to him, 'Lord, how often will my brother sin against me, and I forgive him? As many as seven times?' Jesus said to him, 'I do not say to you seven times, but seventy times seven'"* (Matt. 18:21-22). Christians are to forgive and keep on forgiving.

Whether or not we forgive a brother or sister in Christ affects our prayer life. *"And whenever you stand praying, forgive, if you have anything against anyone, so that your Father also who is in heaven may forgive you your trespasses"* (Mark 11:25). What is the secondary meaning of forgiveness? It means "to let go." We need to let go our hurts, wounds and grudges. We forgive by letting loose the sin that so easily besets us.

Once God has given you the grace to let go of the grudge, then you approach the other person and ask forgiveness.

My older brother was a homosexual, and he died of AIDS. Obviously, my brother and I operated from different views on life. When I was a young, zealous Christian, I said and did some things that deeply offended my brother. I was wrong. My brother and I drifted apart for many years. One day, God convicted me of this estranged relationship. I knew my brother needed forgiveness from God for his lifestyle, but I was convicted that I needed to go to my brother and ask forgiveness for the wrong things I said, and for being indifferent to him all these years. I went to my brother, who was not a Christian, and asked his forgiveness. He was stunned, but that was the beginning of a restored relationship. My brother allowed me to tell him about Christ on his deathbed, though as far as I know he never received Christ as his Savior and Lord. After restoring that relationship, I could lay my head on my pillow and sleep well, knowing that a broken relationship had been restored.

What happens if you are offended by someone, and it causes you deep emotional pain, but God in His grace allows you to forgive this person in your own mind? However, when you go to the person and ask his forgiveness for anything you did wrong, the person will not give you forgiveness. If the person will not give forgiveness, you must go on living. You must let it go. The problem is no longer yours, but the person who refuses to give forgiveness. You continue to pray and ask God to change the person's heart.

As far as I know, I have only one strained relationship in this world. About seven years ago, I apparently said something that offended one of my dearest Christian friends. He perceived I said something that I have no recollection of saying. He broke off fellowship with me, and will not restore that fellowship until I repent. I have called him on the phone. I have written him letters, asking him for forgiveness for something I said or he perceived that I said. He will not bend. My wife, my pastor, my pastor peers have all told me to let it go. I have done everything I could. However, it still bothers me. I do not want to die strained with a Christian brother. Yet, until God changes his heart, I just have to let it go, and go on with my life. I am sure the issue will be resolved at the judgment seat of Christ.

CONCLUSION

Christian, please try to understand that relationships are all that really matter in this world—one's relationship with the Creator, with Christ, with a spouse, with children and grandchildren, with brothers and sisters, and with extended family. Certainly, one's relationship with brothers and sisters in Christ is essential for spiritual health. For any relationship to be meaningful, strong, and dynamic, there must be forgiveness. Forgiveness is hard work and risks being hurt again and again.

If you are estranged or even a little strained with your wife, your husband, your children, your extended family, your unsaved neighbor, or your brother or sister in Christ, go today and right that relationship. Put away your pride, ask for forgiveness, and trust God to do a miracle. It is important to be doctrinally pure, but it is more important to be relationally pure, and that comes only through a genuine, humble attitude of forgiveness.

You say, "I can't do it! There is too much hurt, anger, and distrust in my soul." Yes, you can. You can't do it on your own, but Christ can give you the power to forgive. Remember, if Christ forgave you, He can forgive anyone. Because you are eternally forgiven, you must and can forgive those who sin against you.

QUESTIONS:

1. From what you have learned from this chapter and from your study of the Bible, how would you now define the word "forgiveness?"
2. What does the Bible say about the depth of our sin and our need for forgiveness?
3. What is the attitude of God's heart toward our forgiveness, and what means does He use to bring about this forgiveness? Write out a few talking points for sharing this with someone this week.
4. How would you explain to someone else how your forgiveness of others reflects your understanding of God's forgiveness of you?

chapter 10:
reconciliation

OBJECTIVES

- To know how the Bible uses the word "reconciliation."
- To grasp our great need to be reconciled to God along with our inability to attain this on our own.
- To understand and rely on God's basis for reconciling us to Him.
- To know the changes that reconciliation should make so that you will seek to have such fruit in your life.

"Why am I so unhappy? Why don't I have peace within me? Why am I unsettled and insecure in my heart about life?" These are the kinds of questions I hear from people who are searching for answers to life. These people often go on to tell me they have money, success, prestige, and education, but they still know nothing of inward peace. Why?

The answer I give to these people may seem simplistic, but I believe it gets to the heart of the problem. I tell them that men need to be at peace with God. Until a man is at peace with God, there is no basis for peace in any other phase of life. The doctrine of reconciliation deals with the subject of how men can be at peace with God.

DEFINITION OF RECONCILIATION

The word "reconciliation" comes from the Latin and means "to bring a person again into friendly relations to or with oneself or another after estrangement." The Greek word for "reconciliation" is from the verb *apollasso* which means "to change completely from an enemy to a friend." Reconciliation, in its biblical and theological sense, is a finished work of God whereby sinful man is brought, by the death of Christ, from a position and attitude of being an enemy to a position and attitude of being a friend. The cross brings a sinner from a position of enmity to a position of amity.

Note that "reconciliation" is never used of God. It is used only of man. Reconciliation is manward, for it is sinful men who need to be reconciled to God. God is the reconciler and man is the reconciled.

Reconciliation is totally an act of God. He took the initiative to reconcile the sinner. When we think of a couple about to seek a divorce, but change their minds and come back to one another, we say they were reconciled. This decision was a fifty-fifty proposition by both parties. However, biblical reconciliation is not like this. It is a one hundred percent effort of God to reconcile sinful men to Himself. God restores the ruptured relationship between Himself and rebellious man. God's ways are not our ways and He has reconciled us to teach us much about His love, grace, and mercy.

NEED FOR RECONCILIATION

God does not have to be reconciled to man because God is love. Man has to be reconciled to God because man is a helpless enemy of God. *"For if while we were enemies we were reconciled to God by the death of his Son, much more, now that we are reconciled, shall we be saved by his life"* (Rom. 5:10). All men, because of the fall of Adam and Eve, are sinners by imputation, nature, and acts. Men have a position as sinners before God that makes them enemies of God. Man's legal position (his state, condition, and relationship to God) is that of His enemy. Objectively, in the sight of God, all men are born into this world as enemies and hostile to the one, true, and living God.

D. Martin Lloyd-Jones, in his commentary on Romans, says,

> The terms "technical" and "legal" can be explained by an analogy. We talk about countries being "at war" with one another or in a "state of war." Before they come to that, very often they break off diplomatic relationship; but still they are not technically in a state of war. They have to take another step before they are actually at war; they have to declare war. It is only then that the two countries are technically and legally at war. They are now enemies and in a state of war. That is the position which the Apostle is describing here. He is not so much concerned at this point—and I will be able to demonstrate this—with our feelings of enmity against God. What he is saying is that the mutual relationship and attitude is one of war and of enmity. We were in this position, this legal position, of being enemies of God. God looked upon us as enemies, and we were at enmity against God. The Apostle is concerned with the whole relationship and state and not with our subjective feelings.

Man's objective position, however, as an enemy of God affects his subjective attitude toward the one, true, and living God. Man's heart is estranged and alienated from God. The unsaved man is consciously hostile to God and His law. *"For the mind that is set on the flesh is hostile to God, for it does not submit to God's law; indeed, it cannot. Those who are in the flesh cannot please God"* (Rom. 8:7-8). The natural man is at war with Deity; he hates God and the authority of God. He exerts his own independence from God. Man is in rebellion to God, and has declared his selfwill before God.

You may be saying, "I don't feel like I am an enemy of God. I don't murder, commit adultery, get drunk, cheat, or steal. Surely I am not as bad a person as the Bible declares I am." Yes, you are! The very worst sin of all is selfishness. You want your own way, and all other sins are the outgrowth of this one root sin. *"All we like sheep have gone astray; we have turned every one to his own way"* (Isa. 53:6a). Your natural way is always hostile to God's way. You are an enemy because you want your own way instead of God's way. You probably are not a total rejecter of God but you want God on your terms rather than His. You are a rebel because you will not bow your will to the sovereign God and His holy law as it is revealed in the Bible. You do not have to be an atheist or a communist to be an enemy of God. You do not have to be an idolater who worships idols of sticks and stones to be hostile to God. Anyone who denies God or perverts God or makes a god of his own imagination is an enemy of God. It is possible to be within the pale of Christendom and be an idolater, for an idol is any substitute for God. Even a person within the confines of a local church could have money as his god, or worship prestige, or bow down to the god of sex or pleasure, or do homage to the god of respectability. This person is an enemy of God. Why? Because he wants his way and not God's way! Think about this for a moment. If a person does not believe God's Word as it is revealed in the Bible, this makes a person a pure enemy of God, for he says God is a liar. O vain man, do you not see your rebellion, innate hatred, subtle opposition, and basic hostility to the one true God? Yes, you are an enemy of God whether you believe it or not. You are in desperate need to be reconciled to God or you shall perish in your sins and face an angry God in eternity.

FACT OF RECONCILIATION

The Bible makes it clear that while we were yet in the position of enemies, God moved toward us. He took the initiative to reconcile us. *"For if while we were enemies we were reconciled to God by the death of his Son, much more, now that we are reconciled, shall we be saved by his life. More than that, we also rejoice in God through our Lord Jesus Christ, through whom we have now received reconciliation"* (Rom. 5:10-11). God has reconciled us. Through the death of Christ, we have been brought from an enemy of God to a friend of God, from a position of enmity to a position of amity. God gave us power for our helplessness! He gave us His godliness for our sinfulness, and He gave us His love for our enmity!

95

Because God reconciled the sinner at the cross, this change of position effects a subjective change of attitude in the sinner who responds to Jesus Christ, the Peacemaker. Because of what Christ did for us at the cross, we were enabled to stop hating God, to cease feeling enmity toward Him, and to have our attitudes changed so that we began loving, obeying, and worshiping Him. Why was this all possible? Because of the objective work of reconciliation on the cross for us.

BASIS OF RECONCILIATION

The New Testament declares over and over that the blood of Christ, His substitutionary sacrifice for sin, is the only basis for reconciliation. *"And through him to reconcile to himself all things, whether on earth or in heaven, making peace by the blood of his cross"* (Col. 1:20). *"He has now reconciled in his body of flesh by his death, in order to present you holy and blameless and above reproach before him"* (Col. 1:22). *"For he himself is our peace, who has made us both one and has broken down in his flesh the dividing wall of hostility"* (Eph. 2:14). *"For if while we were enemies we were reconciled to God by the death of his Son, much more, now that we are reconciled, shall we be saved by his life"* (Rom. 5:10). The shedding of Christ's blood as a substitutionary death for sinners is essential to our being made God's friends. The shedding of Christ's blood is the only way God could reconcile sinners to Himself. Many people hate what they call the "theology of the blood," but there is no reconciliation apart from the shed blood of Christ. Christ's death reconciled us.

D. L. Moody often illustrated reconciliation by this story:

A boy quarreled with his father. It was all the boy's fault. The father held nothing against the son, but the boy left home in anger. He corresponded with his mother and she begged him by letter to come home and be reconciled with his father, but he would not. Then one day the son received a letter that his mother was very sick and later received a telegram that his mother was dying. The son hurried home to be beside his mother in her death. When he got home, he hurried up the stairs to the room where he knew his mother was near death. There on the opposite side of the bed stood his father. The boy wouldn't talk or look at his father. His mother pled for him to be reconciled to his father but he refused. Finally the mother took the right hand of the boy in her right hand, and the right hand of the father in her left hand. She put the two hands together over her breast and asked them to be reconciled, and then she fell back on the pillow dead. Then the boy looked up and said, "Father!" These two were reconciled by the death of the mother. The same happened at Calvary. The Lord Jesus reconciled sinners to the Father through His death for sin.

A belief in the blood of Christ is essential to salvation. You may declare that God is love and no longer your enemy; you may determine to turn over a new leaf so as to be less hostile to God; you may understand you are an enemy of God and choose to have a more moral life— but if you do not see that you are utterly dependent on the death of God's Son, the blood of Christ, you shall never be reconciled to God, for only the blood of Christ can bring you from an enemy to a friend.

EFFECTS OF RECONCILIATION

Knowledge that all those who have trusted in Christ are reconciled to God through the death of Christ should have a definite effect on the way we live and the things we do as Christians. The doctrine of reconciliation has practical effects for everyday Christian living.

BASIS OF ASSURANCE

> For if while we were enemies we were reconciled to God by the death of his Son, much more, now that we are reconciled, shall we be saved by his life. (Rom. 5:10)

This is an argument from the greater to the lesser. If God did the hardest thing by reconciling us to Himself when we were sinners and enemies, will He not be able to do the lesser thing: save us by Christ's life? Since God reconciled us, will He not also take us into eternity? Yes, and this is the basis for our hope and assurance of salvation.

BASIS OF EXALTATION

> More than that, we also rejoice in God through our Lord Jesus Christ, through whom we have now received reconciliation. (Rom. 5:11)

A knowledge that the Christian has been reconciled, and will be glorified, should cause great rejoicing and exaltation. The Christian rejoices exultantly in God for His perfect work of salvation in Christ. This verse tells us that Christians should be excited about their salvation. The wonder of being a friend of God, when we deserved nothing, should captivate our thinking and keep our hearts warm.

BASIS OF PEACE IN THE CHURCH

> But now in Christ Jesus you who once were far off have been brought near by the blood of Christ. For he himself is our peace, who has made us both one and has broken down in his flesh the dividing wall of hostility by abolishing the law of commandments

and ordinances, that he might create in himself one new man in place of the two, so making peace, and might reconcile us both to God in one body through the cross, thereby killing the hostility. (Eph. 2:1316)

Christ in His death has broken down the middle wall of partition between Jews and Gentiles. Now both Jews and Gentiles can be reconciled to God on the same basis: faith in the Lord Jesus Christ. Both Jews and Gentiles have equal spiritual privilege and form one body, the church. Christ put to death all enmity and brought peace through His death for sinful men.

This same principle applies in the church today. Every Christian is to be accepted in the body because all Christians have been reconciled to God through Christ and are friends of God. No other Christian should ever be our enemy, and all Christians should be our friends because we are all friends of God.

BASIS FOR HOLY LIVING

And through him to reconcile to himself all things, whether on earth or in heaven, making peace by the blood of his cross. And you, who once were alienated and hostile in mind, doing evil deeds, he has now reconciled in his body of flesh by his death, in order to present you holy and blameless and above reproach before him. (Col. 1:20-22)

Christ reconciled us when we were alienated and hostile to God for the purpose of one day presenting us holy, blameless, and beyond reproach before God. This is our ultimate goal: Christ-likeness. However, we can experience holiness to some degree now in this life as we walk close to Christ and do His will daily. God changed us from an enemy to a friend, and now we shall love Him and serve Him because He is our friend.

BASIS FOR PREACHING THE GOSPEL

All this is from God, who through Christ reconciled us to himself and gave us the ministry of reconciliation; that is, in Christ God was reconciling the world to himself, not counting their trespasses against them, and entrusting to us the message of reconciliation. Therefore, we are ambassadors for Christ, God making his appeal through us. We implore you on behalf of Christ, be reconciled to God. For our sake he made him to be sin who knew no sin, so that in him we might become the righteousness of God. (2 Corinthians 5:18-21)

The first thing to notice is that *"all this is from God."* The whole salvation process flows from God's sovereign purposes. If we are reconciled today, it is because God purposed it to be so. *"Who through Christ reconciled us to Himself."*

Those who have been reconciled by God through Christ are given the ministry of proclaiming reconciliation to the lost world. *"And gave us the ministry of reconciliation."* We Christians have been entrusted with the Gospel. It is our ministry to understand the Gospel and to proclaim it accurately to the world. The message of reconciliation is: *"In Christ God was reconciling the world to Himself, not counting their trespasses against them."* The message is that anyone in the world can be changed from an enemy of God to a friend of God by faith in Christ who died for sinners. *"For our sake he made him to be sin who knew no sin, so that in him we might become the righteousness of God."* Christ was made sin for the sinner, and all the sinner has to do is believe that this is true. Again, the message of reconciliation has been committed to those who have been reconciled. He was *"entrusting to us the message of reconciliation."* No more are going to be reconciled to God then those to whom we are willing to take the Gospel. Our task is to faithfully take the Gospel to all men, inviting them to receive Jesus Christ.

Christians are ambassadors for Christ and are to plead with the unsaved world to be reconciled to God. *"Therefore, we are ambassadors for Christ, God making his appeal through us. We implore you on behalf of Christ, be reconciled to God."* An ambassador speaks on behalf of his sovereign or government. His whole responsibility is to interpret his ruler's or government's mind correctly and to factually give this message out. Christians are to proclaim the Gospel facts and promises to the lost world, and urge sinners to receive the reconciliation effected at the cross. The Christian is merely a man with a message. He is God's mouthpiece, herald, spokesman, and ambassador. He derives his authority from God and will not modify or compromise God's message of reconciliation to please men. Every Christian has a message for this world: *"Be reconciled to God!"*

EXTENT OF RECONCILIATION

In Christ God was reconciling the world to himself, not counting their trespasses against them." (2 Cor. 5:19)

Does this verse teach that Christ provisionally made all man without exception reconcilable, or does it teach that Christ actually reconciled some men, the elect of God? Those who believe in unlimited atonement hold that Christ made a provision for the reconciliation of the whole world in a positional sense (Christ's death has rendered all men savable and broken down every human barrier for men to be saved), but the death of Christ is applied only to those who believe (the elect). They appeal to 2 Cor. 5:19. Those who believe in limited atonement (my own position) are quick to point out the following things: The context clearly says that the "world" does not have their sins charged to their account. If this refers to the world of mankind, then every man has his sins charged to Christ, which is universalism (all will be ultimately saved). The "world," therefore, is not all men in general, but all in the world who lay hold of Christ by faith. The term "world" is qualified by the statement "not counting their trespasses against them." Since there is a "world of the ungodly"—**"[God] did not spare the ancient world, but preserved Noah, a herald of righteousness, with seven others, when he brought a flood upon the world of the ungodly"** (2 Peter 2:5) — and they are lost because they bear their own sins, then it is not illogical that there is a "believing world" who do not have their sins imputed to them but to Christ. This refers to the elect, and the context bears this out. *"For our sake he made him to be sin who knew no sin, so that in him we might become the righteousness of God."* (2 Cor. 5:21)

The context also tells us that Christ is not the sin-bearer for all men indiscriminately, for some are reconciled to God and some are not: *"reconciled us [believers]"* and *"you [unbelievers] ... , be reconciled to God."*

THEOLOGICAL PROBLEMS

As soon as a person hears about limited atonement (definite atonement or particular redemption), he superficially concludes that this doctrine will kill one's desire to win souls, for if Christ did not die for everyone then not everyone can be saved.

I have said it in another chapter and I will say it again, that limited atonement will make a person more zealous for souls and more diligent in preaching the Gospel accurately. First, men can be saved only by trusting in Christ and His death for sins; therefore, the death of Christ is to be preached to all men. Second, the death of Christ is for any man who wants to be saved; the problem is that all men do not want to be saved. Third, if we say that we cannot preach the Gospel to all men unless we know that Christ died for all men, then what about election? God has not elected all men to salvation; yet we can preach Christ to them without any reservation. We must leave the sovereign purposes of God with God and preach salvation through faith in Christ to man. Fourth, the death of Christ guarantees that millions and millions of people will be saved. A great host that no man can number will be redeemed and reconciled by the blood of Christ. Fifth, limited atonement (particular redemption) gives great confidence in preaching the Gospel, for this doctrine guarantees that some will come to Christ. Every person for whom Christ died will come to Christ. Every time I preach or share the Gospel, I expect God to save men. Why? Because those for whom Christ died must come. Who are they? Any and every person who lays hold of Jesus Christ by faith.

A young preacher was talking to Charles Spurgeon and lamenting the fact that so few were responding to Christ under his ministry. Spurgeon said to him, "Do you earnestly believe that every single time you talk to someone about Christ that that person will respond?" The young man said, "No." Spurgeon replied, "Then that is your problem."

We must anticipate and await God's saving of people, and that can be done only by a belief in election and particular redemption.

CREEDAL STATEMENTS

Almost all the creeds of the historic church, especially from the Reformation down to the present, have affirmed a belief in the doctrine of limited atonement. This doctrine has been held with tenacity among the best of saints and the strongest of denominations.

Confessions are nothing but doctrinal statements. They express the doctrinal understanding of an individual or groups. The Scots Confession, the Westminster Confession, the London Confession, the Philadelphia Confession, and many other Confessions of Faith speak out for limited atonement (particular redemption, definite atonement).

Westminster Confession (Presbyterian):

The Lord Jesus, by His perfect obedience, and sacrifice of Himself, which He through the eternal Spirit, once offered up unto God, hath fully satisfied the justice of His Father; and purchased not only reconciliation, but an everlasting inheritance in the kingdom of heaven, for all those whom the Father hath given unto Him.

Philadelphia Confession (Baptist):

It pleased God, in His eternal purpose, to choose and ordain the Lord Jesus, His only begotten Son, according to the covenant made between them both, to be the mediator between God and man; the prophet, priest and king; head and Saviour of; the heir of all things, and judge of the world: unto whom he did from all eternity give a people to be his seed, and to be by him in time redeemed, called, justified, sanctified and glorified.

Often it is said by people who are opposed to sovereign grace that Dr. Arnold has left the faith by believing so strongly in election, predestination, and definite atonement. My rebuttal is that today's evangelicals have left the biblical and historical faith in the major areas of theology. My position stands on the Bible and is reinforced by the historic creeds of Protestantism. I am convinced that every day the church of Jesus Christ grows weaker because Christians are leaving or compromising the truths that God the Father elects men to salvation; God the Son redeems the elect; and God the Holy Spirit applies the death of Christ to the elect. I stand on these truths. God help us all to stand!

CONCLUSION

Man does not want God's authority over him. He is a rebel, and rebels can have no peace. An enemy of God has no rest day or night. How can he get peace? How can he be made a friend of God? How can he be reconciled to God? By sheathing his sword, laying down his weapons and stopping the fighting against God, and accepting the fact that Christ died for him to reconcile him to God. By faith he must accept Christ who made peace between God and man, trusting Christ, the Peacemaker, and finding peace with God.

QUESTIONS:

1. From what you have learned from this chapter and from your study of the Bible, how would you define the word "reconciliation"?

2. What does the Bible say about our need to be reconciled to God and our ability (or lack thereof) to accomplish it?

3. What would you tell someone else about the basis for God's reconciliation of us to Him?

4. Write an outline of what you would say to someone who wants to know the differences it should make in everyday life that he or she is reconciled to God. Look for an opportunity this week to share this.

chapter 11:
propitiation

OBJECTIVES

- To know what the Bible means by the term "propitiation."
- To grasp the importance of a biblical understanding of propitiation for knowing who God is and what He has done for us.
- To make the connection between the Old Testament sacrificial system, especially the Day of Atonement, and the suffering of God's wrath by Jesus Christ.
- To defend the biblical picture of propitiation against objections.

Why did Christ die? Most Christians would say, "He died to deliver me from my sins." It is very natural to look at the atonement in terms of the benefits we receive. Most people say, "What can the death of Christ do for me?" They probably never ask, "What did the death of Christ do for God the Father?"

Most people think the main purpose of the death of Christ was to bring sinful men to God. However, I would suggest that there was an even greater problem solved in the atoning work of Jesus Christ. This problem, which was solved at the cross, was how to bring a holy, righteous, and just God to sinful men. The doctrine of propitiation explains how God can have fellowship with men.

PROPITIATION DEFINED

The basic meaning of propitiation is "to appease" or "to satisfy." Propitiation is God-ward, for it is God, not man, who needs to be propitiated. Biblically speaking, propitiation is the appeasing of the wrath of God and the satisfying of His holy, righteous demands against sin.

Why does God need to be appeased? God is angry with sin and sinners. *"God is a righteous judge, and a God who feels indignation every day"* (Psa. 7:11). God in His nature is holy and righteous, and can have no fellowship with sin and sinners. He must judge all sin because He is a God of absolute justice. *"For you are not a God who delights in wickedness; evil may not dwell with you. The boastful shall not stand before your eyes; you hate all evildoers"* (Psa. 5:4-5). *"For the wrath of God is revealed from heaven against all ungodliness and unrighteousness of men, who by their unrighteousness suppress the truth"* (Rom. 1:18). It is a revealed fact, not a matter of opinion or argument, that God hates sinners and His holy wrath is revealed from heaven against sin. God's wrath against sinful men must be appeased or He will judge them for all eternity, because He is a consuming fire.

All men are sinners—by nature, by imputation, and by acts—and have broken God's moral law. Men are indifferent to the Creator and rebels against God, and live independently of the Lord. Man deserves the anger, wrath, and judgment of God. It matters not what unbelievers may say or think about God's wrath and anger. A just God will judge sin. If God's holy, righteous demands against sin are not satisfied, all sinful men will perish for all eternity.

PROPITIATION IN THE OLD TESTAMENT

Christ's propitiatory sacrifice for sin will never be understood until it is related to the Old Testament animal sacrifices for sin. While the animal sacrifices temporarily covered sin and were the basis for forgiveness until Christ should come and die, the primary design of Old Testament animal sacrifices was to propitiate God. These sacrifices were not meant to affect man, but were directed toward God. Their design was to appease and satisfy God's holy wrath against sin.

Propitiation is best portrayed in the Old Testament by the Day of Atonement, the most significant feast day for Israel. On that day, the high priest entered the Holy of Holies in the Tabernacle to make an atonement for the nation of Israel. *"For on this day shall atonement be made for you to cleanse you. You shall be clean before the LORD from all your sins"* (Lev. 16:30). God dwelt in the Holy of Holies in His Shekinah Glory. No man was allowed in the Holy of Holies except the high priest, and he could go only on the Day of Atonement.

In the Holy of Holies stood only the Ark of the Covenant. The Ark contained three articles: (1) a pot of manna, (2) Aaron's rod that budded, and (3) tablets of the Ten Commandments. On the Ark was the Mercy Seat which had two golden cherubim (angels) on each side looking down on the Mercy Seat. Above the Mercy Seat was the pillar of cloud and smoke that was the Shekinah Glory. This is where God dwelt.

The Ten Commandments represented the fact that all men had broken God's law and were sinners. The Shekinah Glory represented the holiness of God. The Mercy Seat stood between sinful man and a holy God.

The Day of Atonement was a dramatic moment for Israel. On this unique day the high priest would put on special garments of white and undergo ceremonial purification to offer this sacrifice for the sins of ignorance committed by the children of Israel during the previous year.

The high priest offered the sacrifice of a bull for himself and a goat for Israel. The people would watch the animals killed and the blood taken into the Tabernacle. The high priest would move through the Holy Place with the bowl of blood in one hand and a censor of fire in the other hand. When he got to the veil that separated the Holy Place from the Holy of Holies, he would stop and strip himself of his white robe down to his tunic, indicating that sinful man is spiritually naked before a holy God. Then he would push back the veil. Surely this was a tense moment. He would be frightened, anxious, and nervous, for he would not know what he would meet behind the veil. He then put down the censor of fire and threw special incense on it so as to fill the room with smoke. This was done because the Bible says that no man can look upon God and live. Slowly the high priest would move toward the Mercy Seat, having a cord tied to one leg in case he should make a mistake and God would strike him dead. The other priests could then pull him out of the Holy of Holies without entering themselves. Then the high priest would sprinkle the blood—one time toward heaven and seven times on the Mercy Seat. If God did not display His anger, the priest would know that God was appeased and Israel's sins were covered for another year.

The congregation of Israel would watch with breathless anticipation as they saw the high priest take the blood into the Tabernacle to sprinkle it on the Mercy Seat. The questions every Israelite would ask were, "Will God accept this sacrifice? Will our sins be covered another year? Will God bring immediate judgment on us because of our sins?" The people, filled with excitement and anticipation, would see the high priest come out of the Tabernacle and they would breathe a sigh of relief because they knew that God's wrath had been appeased for another year and they need not fear His judgment.

PROPITIATION FULFILLED IN CHRIST

For all have sinned and fall short of the glory of God, and are justified by his grace as a gift, through the redemption that is in Christ Jesus, whom God put forward as a propitiation by his blood, to be received by faith. This was to show God's righteousness, because in his divine forbearance he had passed over former sins. It was to show his righteousness at the present time, so that he might be just and the justifier of the one who has faith in Jesus. (Rom. 3:23-26)

The New Testament declares *"Christ Jesus, whom God put forward as a propitiation by his blood, to be received by faith"* (Rom. 3:24b-25). Jesus Christ is the Christian's Mercy Seat. Christ's death propitiated, appeased, and satisfied the holy righteous demands of God against sin. This sacrifice could be made only by Christ, the Lamb without spot or blemish, whose blood was spilled for sinners. God the Father was perfectly satisfied with the death of Christ. The cross satisfied once and for all God's holy wrath and anger against men. Christ's death is the only meeting place between God and man. God forgives sins and holds back wrath only from those who are covered by the blood of Christ.

No mere man could produce an acceptable sacrifice to God. The whole glory of the Gospel is that God Himself has provided this propitiatory sacrifice. God, in love, sent His Son Jesus Christ to be the perfect sacrifice for sin. The very God whom we offended has Himself provided the substitute in Jesus Christ, who was perfectly human and truly divine. Christ became the sinner's substitute and propitiatory sacrifice. This gives us a glimpse into God's great love toward us!

When the Bible declares that God *"gave His only Son"* (John 3:16) and *"gave Him up for us all"* (Rom. 8:32), does it mean that God simply allowed Christ to die? No! God poured out His wrath against sin on the person of Jesus Christ. God's punishment and judgment were placed directly on Jesus Christ. God did not spare His Son from His own anger, wrath, and punishment. This is why Christ faced deep agony in the Garden of Gethsemane and sweated great drops of blood. He pleaded with the Father, *"My Father, if it be possible, let this cup pass from me"* (Matt. 26:39).

Christ did not fear mere physical death. Many martyrs have not flinched at suffering and death, dying gladly and boldly. Christ was contemplating being the direct object of God's holy anger and wrath. This is what caused Christ to cry out on the cross, *"My God, my God, why have you forsaken me?"* (Matt. 27:46). He who was perfect in act and thought was experiencing God's wrath and anger against sin. He was separated from His Father. God took His anger out on Christ instead of sinners. He put His punishment of hell on Christ instead of sinners! Because of propitiation, anyone who will place his faith and trust in Jesus Christ as personal Savior from sin will receive the forgiveness of sins, and the wrath of God will never come down on that one. Christ bore the wrath of God for that person. Why? Because Christ satisfied the holy, righteous demands of God against sin. Now, through the death of Christ, a holy God and a sinful man can meet, and God can have fellowship with men.

PROPITIATION APPLIED BY THE CHRISTIAN

Propitiation, like every other doctrine of the Bible, has direct ramifications to the Christian. Doctrine is always practical and must be applied to life by faith. Propitiation affects the way we live as believers in the Lord Jesus Christ.

The Christian now has a strong evangelical message to the world of unbelievers. God has been propitiated (satisfied, appeased) in Christ. God can now *"be just and the justifier of the one who has faith in Jesus"* (Rom. 3:26). God is just and holy, and He must judge sin and the sinner or He would not be God. His wrath and anger must still find an outlet against the terribleness of sin and sinners. God is absolutely just in judging sin. However, in the death of Christ, God has solved the sin problem. God, in love, has devised a way in which He can justify or declare men righteous. His solution was and is the death of Christ for sin, whereby God poured out His wrath on Christ, who did not deserve it, instead of sinners, who most certainly did deserve it. Justification is open to anyone *"who has faith in Jesus."* This is s super message to give to a lost and dying world under God's judgment.

Propitiation also gives the Christian a strong security that when he sins, Christ's death continues to propitiate God. God does not place His wrath and anger on the true child of God. *"My little children, I am writing these things to you so that you may not sin. But if anyone does sin, we have an advocate with the Father, Jesus Christ the righteous. He is the propitiation for our sins, and not for ours only but also for the sins of the whole world"* (1 John 2:1-2). God desires for Christians not to sin. But, realistically, Christians still do acts of sin. This verse tells us that God has made provision for those sins in the death of Christ. Christ is our advocate or defense lawyer, pleading His perfect and complete death before the throne of the Father.

God's holiness, justice, and righteousness demand that God judge sin, but Christ in His death appeased or satisfied the holy righteous demands of God against sin. Now God cannot judge Christians because He has judged Christ in their place. Christ does not plead the Christian's innocence but His own death, which has brought a perfect salvation to the believer in Christ.

Try to imagine a courtroom scene in heaven with God the Father as the Judge, Christ as the defense lawyer, the Christian as the accused, and the devil as the accuser. When God , the Judge of all, sees the Christian's sin, His holy wrath is stirred. The devil steps forward and says, "God, that Christian is guilty and deserving of your wrath!" Christ immediately comes to the defense of the Christian. He steps up to the heavenly bench and says, "Father, I shed my blood to satisfy and appease your wrath against this Christian." The devil cries louder, "Judge him! Judge him!" Christ says, "Father, you cannot judge that Christian because he is covered by my precious blood." The Father, Judge of heaven and earth, says, "Case dismissed!"

Propitiation is also the grounds on which we can love our Christian brothers and sisters. *"In this the love of God was made manifest among us, that God sent his only Son into the world, so that we might live through him. In this is love, not that we have loved God but that he loved us and sent his Son to be the propitiation for our sins. Beloved, if God so loved us, we also ought to love one another"* (1 John 4:9-11). God first loved us when we were sinners and sent His Son to die for us. Christ appeased God's wrath so that He is not angry or wrathful toward any true Christians. Since God first loved us and is not angry with us, then we should not be angry with any of our brothers and sisters in Christ. We should love them because God loves them. Anger against another brother or sister is inconsistent with the whole concept of propitiation.

PROPITIATION LIMITED IN EXTENT

My little children, I am writing these things to you so that you may not sin. But if anyone does sin, we have an advocate with the Father, Jesus Christ the righteous. He is the propitiation for our sins, and not for ours only but also for the sins of the whole world. (1 John 2:1-2)

Did Christ propitiate God the Father on behalf of all men in general or for some men in particular? Did He appease God's wrath and anger against all men indiscriminately or for only the elect of God? Did He satisfy the holy righteous demands against sin for every son of Adam or only for those who put their faith in Christ? I suggest that Christ made satisfaction to the Father on behalf of His elect seed, particularly and definitely.

If it is true that propitiation is limited, then how does one interpret 1 John 2:2? That verse says, *"He is the propitiation for our sins, and not for ours only but also for the sins of the whole world."* At first glance this seems to indicate that Christ's propitiation to the Father extended beyond the elect community, but deeper examination finds that this is not so.

First John 2:2 in the Greek begins with "and" (*kai*) which links it with verse one. Verse one is about Christians and has nothing to say about unbelievers. The primary thought of verse one is the advocacy of Christ for believers. Christians may take comfort in the fact that Christ is their advocate when they sin, because Christ is *"the propitiation for our sins."* There is a definite link between "advocate" and "propitiation." The context deals with Christians, and Christ can be a propitiation for no more than those for whom He is an advocate. Therefore, the term "whole world" is somehow connected with believers. If Christ is a propitiation for all mankind, He surely is an advocate for all mankind, which would teach universalism.

The "our" refers to the apostles and John in particular, and it also refers to all to whom John was writing this book (primarily Hebrew Christians). The "our," therefore, refers to believers. Christ is also a propitiation for the "whole world"; that is, His death is effective to all Jews and Gentiles in the world who believe in Christ. The Jews, even Jews converted to Christ, had to understand that the death of Christ was for anyone in the world who wanted it, Jew or Gentile. The atonement is ethnically universal. Christ is Savior not only for the Jews, but also for the Gentiles.

This verse is very closely connected with the prophecy of Caiaphas concerning the death of Christ for believing Israelites and Gentiles. *"But one of [the council], Caiaphas, who was high priest that year, said to them, 'You know nothing at all. Nor do you understand that it is better for you that one man should die for the people, not that the whole nation should perish.' He did not say this of his own accord, but being high priest that year he prophesied that Jesus would die for the nation, and not for the nation only, but also to gather into one the children of God who are scattered abroad"* (John 11:49-52).

"Whole world" in 1 John 2:2 must be given a limited meaning and refer to all who believe, or the elect. The Apostle John often limits the meaning of "whole world." *"We know that we are from God, and the whole world lies in the power of the evil one"* (1 John 5:19). This may seem to indicate that the whole world is controlled by the wicked one, the devil, but further reflection shows that this is not true. Christians do not lie in the lap of the wicked one. Therefore, this means all in the world *except* true Christians.

In all other passages where propitiation is mentioned, the context limits it to the elect of God. Hebrews 2:17 says, *"Therefore he had to be made like his brothers in every respect, so that he might become a merciful and faithful high priest in the service of God, to make propitiation for the sins of the people"*— not the whole world but God's people. Romans 3:23-25 says, *"For all have sinned and fall short of the glory of God, and are justified by his grace as a gift, through the redemption that is in Christ Jesus, whom God put forward as a propitiation by his blood, to be received by faith."* God's anger is appeased only for those who believe in Jesus Christ. First John 4:10 says God *"loved us and sent his Son to be the propitiation for our sins,"* limiting it to those whom God loved first, the elect of God. Therefore, we conclude that when John says, *"He is the propitiation for our sins, and not for ours only but also for the sins of the whole world"* (1 John 2:2), he is referring to all those in the world who had believed in Christ or were yet to believe in Christ.

As you look at the picture of the Old Testament sacrifice for the Day of Atonement, ask yourself whether the high priest was atoning for the sins only of Israel, or also for the sins of the Canaanites, Hittites, Girgashites, Amorites, Perizzites, Hivites, and Jebusites. The verses below all refer to the propitiation as appeasing the wrath of God against Israel, not the whole world:

> *Thus he shall make atonement for the Holy Place, because of the uncleannesses of the people of Israel and because of their transgressions, all their sins. And so he shall do for the tent of meeting, which dwells with them in the midst of their uncleannesses. No one may be in the tent of meeting from the time he enters to make atonement in the Holy Place until he comes out and has made atonement for himself and for his house and for all the assembly of Israel. (Lev. 16:16-17)*

> *And Aaron shall lay both his hands on the head of the live goat, and confess over it all the iniquities of the people of Israel, and all their transgressions, all their sins. ... Then Aaron shall come into the tent of meeting and shall take off the linen garments that he put on when he went into the Holy Place and shall leave them there. And he shall bathe his body in water in a holy place and put on his garments and come out and offer his burnt offering and the burnt offering of the people and make atonement for himself and for the people. (Lev. 16:21,23-24)*

> *He shall make atonement for the holy sanctuary, and he shall make atonement for the tent of meeting and for the altar, and he shall make atonement for the priests and for all the people of the assembly. (Lev. 16:33)*

Logically, propitiation must be limited to the elect— all who believe. If Christ satisfied God's anger and wrath against all men in general, then God is not angry with all men and His wrath does not burn hot against them. Therefore, there is no judgment and no hell. This would be universalism, and while the logic and reasoning are sound, the Bible rejects universalism and says God's wrath does burn hot against men. *"Whoever believes in the Son has eternal life; whoever does not obey the Son shall not see life, but the wrath of God remains on him"* (John 3:36). Biblically, we should also see the Day of Atonement as a picture (type) of the death of Christ. The blood was sprinkled on the Mercy Seat for all Israel (the covenant people), but not for the world in general. The Gentile nations were not covered by the blood. Christ's death is for all true believers in Christ but not for the whole world.

Therefore, we can conclude that propitiation was made by Christ to appease the wrath of God against the elect seed, particularly and definitely.

CONCLUSION

The Bible says the sinner is separated from God. *"God is a righteous judge, and a God who feels indignation every day"* (Psa. 7:11), and *"The boastful shall not stand before your eyes; you hate all evildoers"* (Psa. 5:5). *"For the wrath of God is revealed from heaven against all ungodliness and unrighteousness of men, who by their unrighteousness suppress the truth"* (Rom. 1:18). This is true whether men believe it or not. God is angry with the sinner because he is in rebellion against God and His law. If a man continues in his independent spirit, doing his own thing, God will most certainly judge him in eternity. This will be a just judgment, for he is guilty before a holy God.

God, however, has planned a way for sinful men to escape the wrath and anger of God. God gave His Son, Jesus Christ, to die as a sinner's substitute and to appease His own wrath against sin. Christ satisfied God's holy and righteous demands against sin, and now any sinner who lays hold of Christ can be set free from the anger and wrath of God forever. Who escapes God's wrath? Only those who receive Christ by faith. Propitiation is in Christ's blood "through faith!"

QUESTIONS:

1. From what you have learned from this chapter and from your study of the Bible, how would you define "propitiation"?
2. What would be the difference in our view of God's character if He simply forgave sins without requiring satisfaction or appeasement of His wrath against sin?
3. Write a letter to someone about what you would say about how the Old Testament Day of Atonement pointed toward the atonement made for us by Jesus Christ. Look for an opportunity this week to share this with someone or mail it to him or her.
4. What would you tell someone about the security that is ours because of Christ's propitiation on our behalf, and how this should affect our love for Christian brothers and sisters?

chapter 12:
death

OBJECTIVES

- To be able to define the issue in the atoning death of Jesus Christ.
- To take to heart the logical arguments for Christ's death being an atonement limited to the elect.
- To grasp the difference between limiting the extent of Christ's atoning death and limiting the extent of its power, and how this difference affects how we view God and live as believers.
- To be able to respond to objections to limited atonement based on the meaning and usage of "all," "every," and "world."

When an evangelical Christian says to a person who is not a Christian, "Christ died for you," has he really thought through that statement, and does he understand what he is saying? What does he mean by "death"? Does he mean Christ's death is sufficient for all? Does he mean Christ's death is available for all? Or does he mean Christ's death is a substitution for all?

No Christian would deny that Christ's death is sufficient for everyone who has ever lived and that it is available to all who will lay hold of it by faith, but the issue is whether Christ's death is a substitution for all. If we say, as do most evangelicals in America, that Christ's death is a substitution for all, we have some deep theological problems which may not be answerable. This kind of theology cracks open the door for universalism (that all men ultimately will be saved).

The issue among evangelical Christians is this: For whom did Christ die? Did He die to save sinners or to render all sinners savable? Did He die for all men in general or for a definite number in particular? Did Christ die to save those He saves, or did He die to save those He does not save? The purpose of this chapter is to show that the Bible teaches a limited extent of the atonement. Sometimes this is called "definite atonement" or "particular redemption." The thrust of this lesson is to show that when Christ hung on the cross, He was dying for His elect seed, personally and definitely.

As Bible-believing evangelicals, we must think deeply about our Christian faith in a day when Christianity is losing its power and momentum. We must give concentrated thought to salvation and what it really means to be saved. We must meditate on the meaning of the cross, so we will not be tossed to and fro by every wind of doctrine.

In this century, our minds have been conditioned because of an increase in free will theology to think of the cross as a means of redemption that does less than save; of God's love as a weak affection that cannot keep anyone from hell without help; and of faith as the human help that God needs for this purpose. Today's evangelical world is unconsciously involved in synergism— that salvation comes about through cooperation between God and man. Why this defect in the modern Gospel? Simply because we do not understand sovereign election and particular redemption as taught in the Bible.

> And when we come to preach the gospel, our false preconceptions make us say just the opposite of what we intend. We want (rightly) to proclaim Christ as Savior; yet we end up saying that Christ, having made salvation possible, has left us to become our own saviors. It comes about in this way. We want to magnify the saving grace of God and the saving power of Christ. So we declare that God's redeeming love extends to every man, and that Christ has died to save every man, and we proclaim that the glory of divine mercy is to be measured by these facts. And then, in order to avoid universalism, we have to depreciate all that we were previously extolling, and to explain that, after all, nothing that God and Christ have done can save us unless we add something to it. The decisive factor which actually saves us is our own believing. What we say comes to this—that Christ saves us with our help; and what that means, when one thinks it out, is this—that we save ourselves with Christ's help. (J. I. Packer, Introductory Essay to John Owen's *The Death of Death in the Death of Christ*)

DEFINING THE ISSUE

The issue is this: for whom did Christ die? All evangelicals believe Christ died for sin and sinners: *"Christ died for our sins in accordance with the Scriptures ..."* (1 Cor. 15:3). *"But God shows his love for us in that while we were still sinners, Christ died for us"* (Rom. 5:8). The issue is whether He died for all sinners in general, or some sinners in particular.

Some evangelical Christians believe in sovereign election but also hold to a universal atonement. They refer to themselves as "Four Point Calvinists." Others, like me, hold to election and a limited atonement, and are known as "Five Point Calvinists." Both believe (1) that there is unconditional election with a countless number of people saved and a countless number of people lost; (2) that the death of Christ is sufficient to save a person from sin and hell; (3) that the Gospel must be preached universally to all men; (4) that only the elect will be saved; (5) that saving faith must be produced in the believer by the Holy Spirit; and (6) that the death of Christ must be applied by the Holy Spirit to the sinner before salvation is complete.

There are, however, differences between a person who holds to sovereign election and unlimited atonement and a person who believes in sovereign election and limited atonement. The issue is over <u>substitution</u>.

Those who believe in limited atonement say that substitution demands a limited extent of the atonement, and that this is consistent with sovereign election. Those who hold to an unlimited atonement have several problems that logically are unanswerable. They are forced logically to see two phases for the atonement, one non-redemptive phase for all mankind and one redemptive phase for those who believe.

Those who hold to unlimited atonement must concede a mystery and ignore the whole concept of substitution. The mystery for them is that Christ died for everyone, but the benefits of His death are applied only to those who believe—the elect. However, it is doubtful that the extent of the atonement can be put into the category of a mystery. Why? Because of substitution.

Substitution means that Christ died "in the place of," "in behalf of," and "in the stead of" sinners, bearing their sin, curse, condemnation, judgment, hell, and unbelief. If Christ substituted for all, then why are not all saved? Furthermore, if Christ died for all, is He so weak He could not save those for whom He substituted?

Do not misunderstand me—there *is* a mystery about the atonement. The mystery, however, is not that Christ died for all men in general and this death is applied only to the elect. The mystery is that Christ died for the elect but the death of Christ is sufficient for, available to, and offered to anyone who wants it by faith. Obviously, there are some things about the atonement we will never understand this side of glory.

LOGICAL ARGUMENT TO
SUPPORT DEFINITE ATONEMENT

Sin of Unbelief

Those who believe in unlimited atonement say that Christ died for the sins of all men, and the only thing keeping a person from salvation is unbelief toward Christ. Is unbelief a sin? Yes, of course it is. If Christ died for <u>all</u> the sins of all men, then did He die for the sin of unbelief? Absolutely. Why then are not all men saved? If Christ did not die for unbelief, then no one is saved.

Those who believe in unlimited redemption must say that Christ died for every sin except unbelief. If this is so, then He did not make a perfect and complete sacrifice for all sin. We are all guilty of unbelief daily!

Unlimited atonement gets one into deep theological water. It is better to limit the extent of the atonement, and say that Christ bore all the sins of all who would ever believe on Him—the elect of God— than to limit the power of the atonement, and say that Christ bore all sins except the sin of unbelief.

Dr. John Owen, chaplain to Oliver Cromwell and vice chancellor of Oxford University, made these piercing observations:

> The Father imposed His wrath due unto, and the Son underwent punishment for, either: (1) All the sins of all men; (2) All the sins of some men, or (3) Some of the sins of all men, in which case it may be said: (1) That if the last be true, all men have some sins to answer for, and so none are saved; (2) That if the second be true, then Christ, in their stead suffered for all the sins of all the elect in the whole world, and this is truth; (3) But if the first be the case, why are not all men free from the punishment due unto their sins? Your answer, Because of unbelief. I ask, is this unbelief a sin, or is it not? If it be, then Christ suffered the punishment due unto it, or He did not. If He did, why must that hinder them more than their other sins for which He died? If He did not, He did not die for all their sins.

Sin Question

Those who believe in unlimited atonement claim that the issue with unsaved men is no longer the sin question but the Son question. The Son has died for every sin of mankind, and now unbelievers should not be concerned about sin but about the Son. However, the Bible states that sin is still very much an issue. *"I told you that you would die in your sins, for unless you believe that I am he you will die in your sins"* (John 8:24).

Men will die in their sins and be judged for all eternity because they have no Savior who substituted for their sins. If Christ has atoned for all sins and removed the sin from all people, how can anyone die in his sins? He can't! Substitution for sin is found only in Christ, and only for the believer.

PAYMENT FOR SIN

Would God be just in demanding payment twice for a debt? Christ did pay the debt for sin. If He paid the debt for every human being, then some men (rejecters of Christ) will pay the debt a second time by suffering in hell. This would make God unjust if he demanded a debt be paid twice.

If we believe in unlimited atonement, we must conclude that men for whom Christ died are in hell today. This would make the death of Christ ineffective in keeping men out of hell. If His death could not keep the unbeliever out of hell, how does anyone know His death will keep the Christian out of hell? It seems as though Christ died in vain if men for whom He died are in hell. This forces the answer to be that it is my faith that keeps me out of hell, and now the salvation issue is revolving around me again instead of around Jesus.

POWER OF THE ATONEMENT

Those who believe in unlimited atonement accuse particular redemptionists of lowering the value of the cross. They say the glories and the power of the cross are minimized if Christ did not die for all men. These are idle words, because the unlimited redemptionist is guilty of a far more serious error than the limited redemptionist. Those who believe in limited atonement limit the extent of the atonement, but the unlimited redemptionist limits the power of the atonement. The cross was powerless to save all men because all men are obviously not saved. An unlimited atonement does not magnify the merit and worth of Christ's death; it cheapens it, for it makes Christ's death powerless. Charles Spurgeon gives us good logic when it comes to the extent of the atonement.

We are often told that we limit the atonement of Christ, because we say that Christ has not made a satisfaction for all men, or all man would be saved. Now, our reply to this is, that, on the other hand, our opponents limit it: we do not. The Arminians say, Christ died for all men. Ask them what they mean by it. Did Christ die so as to secure the salvation of all men? They say, "No, certainly not." We ask them the next question—Did Christ die so as to secure the salvation of any man in particular? They answer, "No." They are obliged to admit this, if they are consistent. They say "No. Christ has died that any man may be saved if"—and then follow certain conditions of salvation. Now, who is it that limits the death of Christ? Why, you. You say that Christ did not die so as infallibly to secure the salvation of anybody. We beg your pardon, when you say we limit Christ's death; we say, "No, my dear sir, it is you that do it." We say Christ so died that he infallibly secured the salvation of a multitude that no man can number, who through Christ's death not only may be saved, but are saved, must be saved and cannot by any possibility run the hazard of being anything but saved. You are welcome to your atonement; you may keep it. We will never renounce ours for the sake of it."

If Christ died only potentially or provisionally for the sins of the whole world, then this is only a hypothetical salvation. Definite atonement says Christ actually saved a people at the cross.

Christ did not win a hypothetical salvation for hypothetical believers, a mere possibility of salvation for any who might possibly believe, but a real salvation for His own chosen people. His precious blood really does "save us all"; the intended effects of His self-offering do in fact follow, just because the Cross was what it was. Its saving power does not depend on faith being added to it: its saving power is such that faith flows from it. The Cross secured the full salvation of all for whom Christ died. "God forbid," therefore, "that I should glory, save in the cross of our Lord Jesus Christ." (J. I. Packer, "Introductory Essay")

NUMBER OF SAVED

Whether a person believes in limited or unlimited atonement, the exact same number are going to be saved. Every evangelical limits the atonement somewhere, or all would be universalists. Strict free-willers say Christ died for all men but His death is available only to those who believe. Electionists who believe in unlimited atonement state that Christ died for all men, but the atonement is limited in application to the elect or those who believe. Electionists who believe in limited atonement say Christ died only for the elect, and the elect are those who believe. Not one more soul is saved in any of these views. Furthermore, definite atonement has far fewer theological problems. The death of Christ works only for those who believe. Unlimited redemptionists cannot show that one more person would be saved than those who believe in a definite atonement. When the final number of the redeemed is counted, they will be the same number.

LOVE OF GOD

Those who believe in unlimited atonement say—as we all do—that God so loved the whole world that He gave His only begotten Son to die for it. But they must face the inconsistency that God loved the world enough to send His Son to die for all, but did not love them enough to save all. What kind of love would this be? It is illogical.

There is a perfect unity in the works and purposes of the Triune God. God has chosen certain men to be saved. Is the design of redemption at odds with God's elective purposes? Was the Son trying to do something that the Father was not going to do anyway? Was the Son seeking to save those whom the Father had not purposed to save? Obviously not, for those chosen by the Father must be redeemed by the Son and regenerated by the Holy Spirit. The doctrine of unlimited atonement leads to chaos and confusion within the economy of the Trinity.

PROBLEM PASSAGES ON DEFINITE ATONEMENT

If you have been following along with me on the limited extent of the atonement, you probably are thinking, "What about those verses in Scripture that say Christ gave Himself a ransom for all, or He tasted death for every man, or He takes away the sin of the world? Can I just ignore these verses, for they seem to indicate that the extent of the atonement is wider than just the elect?" As a teacher, I will not ignore deliberately any passage of Scripture on this subject or any other subject, and I will try to answer many of these problem passages that connect the words "all" or "every" or "world" with the extent of the atonement. My answer may not satisfy everyone but I ask you to think about these passages before you draw any conclusions.

THE WORD "ALL"

When we read the word "all" in the Bible, we must put it in the context of the passage. We should remember that the Bible is written in the language of the people, so when we see the word "all" it does not always mean "all in general" or "all inclusively"; that is to say, the word "all" does not have to mean "every single solitary one." Many times "all" is given a limited meaning in the Bible. According to the Puritan John Owen, "all" has a limited meaning at least 500 times in the Bible.

THE USAGE OF "ALL"

"All" may mean *all of all sorts*, as Christ is "Lord of all" (Acts 10:36), which means all inclusively. "All" may also mean *all of some sorts*. Romans 5:18 indicates that *"one act of righteousness leads to justification and life for all men."* If this refers to all men in general, then we have universalism. The "all," however, refers to the many who are made righteous in Christ—referring to true believers. "All" may also mean *some of all sorts*. In 1 Corinthians 6:12, Paul says, *"'All things are lawful for me,' but not all things are helpful.*" This is speaking only of questionable practices in the Christian life. Murder, adultery, lying, and cheating were not lawful for Paul or any Christian. But some of all sorts of practices were possible for Paul within the total law of God.

– John 12:32

"And I, when I am lifted up from the earth, will draw all people to myself."

This in context refers to Christ's death, and it says all men will be drawn to Him. In the Gospel of John, the word "draw" is always used of an effective drawing to salvation. " *'No one can come to me unless the Father who sent me draws him. And I will raise him up on the last day'"* (John 6:44). The "all" must be put in the context of all who believe, for all men are not saved. Christ, therefore, will save all kinds of people—Jews and Gentiles, rich and poor, educated and uneducated.

– 2 Cor. 5:14-15

"One has died for all, therefore all have died ..."

The immediate context tells us that the "all" refers to those who died in Christ, who are the elect or true believers: *"For the love of Christ controls us."* Furthermore, the context tells us that all for whom Christ died should live to God. *"And he died for all, that those who live might no longer live for themselves but for him who for their sake died and was raised"* (2 Cor. 5:15). These can only be true Christians.

– 1 Cor. 15:22

"For as in Adam all die, so also in Christ shall all be made alive."

Every human being has died in Adam (all without exception). Yet only people "in Christ" shall have spiritual life, and those are the ones for whom Christ died and shares His life. The only ones who die are those in Adam (everyone), and the only ones who are made alive are those in Christ (the elect).

– 1 Tim. 2:5-6

"For there is one God, and there is one mediator between God and men, the man Christ Jesus, who gave himself as a ransom for all..."

This context limits the meaning of "all." In verse one, we are told that prayers are to be made for "all people." In verse two, the "all people" are qualified as *"kings and all who are in high positions."* Therefore, it is accurate to give the meaning of "ransom for all" as all men without distinction or rank, race or nationality. This "all" does not refer to every man without exception but every man without distinction.

THE WORD "EVERY"

Hebrews 2:9 says, *"But we see ... Jesus, crowned with glory and honor because of the suffering of death, so that by the grace of God he might taste death for everyone."* "Everyone" must be taken in context. It refers to "many sons" (2:10), "those who are sanctified" (2:11), "brothers" (2:12), "the children God has given me" (2:13), and "the offspring of Abraham" (2:16). The context limits "everyone" to those who are believers, the elect.

THE WORD "WORLD"

Many times, "world" is qualified by the context of a passage and has a limited meaning. The term "world" (*kosmos*) may mean the universe: *"The God who made the world and everything in it, being Lord of heaven and earth, does not live in temples made by man ..."* (Acts 17:24).

"World" may mean the earth: *"Jesus knew that his hour had come to depart out of this world to the Father, having loved his own who were in the world, he loved them to the end"* (John 13:1).

It may mean the human race: *"Now we know that whatever the law says it speaks to those who are under the law, so that every mouth may be stopped, and the whole world may be held accountable to God"* (Rom. 3:19).

It also may mean the world system: *"Now is the judgment of this world; now will the ruler of this world be cast out"* (John 12:31).

It could mean the Jewish world of Christ's day: *"So the Pharisees said to one another, 'You see that you are gaining nothing. Look, the world has gone after him'"* (John 12:19).

"World" may mean the Roman world of Paul's day: *". . . because your faith is proclaimed in all the world"* (Rom. 1:8). In John 1:10, the term "world" has three different meanings in one verse — earth, universe, and world system: *"He was in the world, and the world was made through him, yet the world did not know him"* (John 1:10). Does the word "world" ever refer to those who believe in Christ? Yes. It refers to the world of believing Gentiles. *"Now if their [Jews'] trespass means riches for the world, and if their failure means riches for the Gentiles, how much more will their full inclusion mean! ... For if their [Jews'] rejection means the reconciliation of the world, what will their acceptance mean but life from the dead?"* (Rom. 11:12,15). The Bible also speaks of a world of unbelievers. *"If he did not spare the ancient world, but preserved Noah, a herald of righteousness, with seven others, when he brought a flood upon the world of the ungodly"* (2 Peter 2:5). Therefore, we can conclude that there is a world of believers. *"For the bread of God [Christ] is he who comes down from heaven and gives life to the world"* (John 6:33). It is obvious that Christ gives life only to those who are true Christians.

– John 1:29

> *"The next day he saw Jesus coming toward him, and said, Behold, the Lamb of God, who takes away the sin of the world!"*

Broad, general, and universal terms such as "world" are used often in the Bible to counteract the horrible Jewish exclusivism of the early first century. Jews thought that salvation was restricted to Jews, and Gentiles had no part in the blessings of salvation. Jews called the Gentiles "dogs," "swine," and "the world". When John the Baptist announced the Lamb of God, he was saying that salvation was for Gentiles as well as Jews. The "world" in this context refers to the world of believers—both Jews and Gentiles.

Notice that John 1:29 says the Lamb of God "takes away the sin of the world." It does not say that Christ tries to take away sin or that He made provision for all sin. He simply takes it away. Therefore, this must refer to the world of believers.

– John 4:42

> *"We know that this is indeed the Savior of the world."*

Christ is the Savior of all men and women in the world who believe. This again is a general term to help Jewish exclusivists to see that the death of Christ is for the whole world, if the world will have it. Christ is *a Savior* for the whole world but is not *the Savior* of the whole world, or the whole world would be saved.

Notice again that this verse says Christ "is the Savior of the world," so this must refer to all in the world who truly believe in Christ.

DOES DEFINITE ATONEMENT
KILL EVANGELISTIC ZEAL?

The most common objection to believing in sovereign election and particular redemption is that it would kill missionary zeal. A glance at church history should lay this objection to rest forever. There have been some particular redemptionists in the history of the church who were dead, lifeless, and cold, but they are the exceptions. If they were inactive for Christ, it was because they had an intellectual understanding of sovereign grace but no heart for the living God.

Almost every (if not every) major revival in the church has had at its base sovereign grace theology. The moving of the Spirit under the apostles in the first century was strongly oriented toward sovereign grace. The Reformation of the sixteenth century was a revival of sovereign grace theology. It was John Calvin who said, "Christ died actually for the elect and potentially for the world." The revivals in Scotland, Wales, and England had at their base sovereign election and particular redemption. The First Great Awakening in America in the 1730s and 1740s had sovereign grace as its foundation.

If a belief in sovereign election and particular redemption kills missionary zeal, then why is it that all the founders of the early missionary societies of the 1780s were electionists? William Carey, who is called the Father of Modern Missions, was a believer in sovereign grace. In America, John Elliott, the Mayhews, and David Brainard took the message of Christ to the Indians, and they were all committed to sovereign grace theology.

Where revival is taking place in the world today, sovereign grace is being taught. In the East Indies, the Dutch Reformed Church has had its influence. In South Korea, the Presbyterians have labored. Whether in East Africa, Uganda, Kenya, Brazil, or Nigeria, the hub of any revivals taking place flows from sovereign grace theology. Not all people involved in these revivals believe in sovereign grace, but they have at its nucleus these doctrines.

It is a misunderstanding to think that belief in particular redemption destroys missionary zeal. Most of the great Christian men in the church have believed in election and particular redemption, including Augustine, Martin Luther, John Calvin, John Knox, John Bunyan, Oliver Cromwell, George Whitefield, Jonathan Edwards, David Brainerd, Charles Spurgeon, J. Gresham Machen, B. B. Warfield, Donald Grey Barnhouse, R. C. Sproul, and a host of others. Probably the leading evangelical theologian-preacher of our day is J. I. Packer, and he is committed to sovereign grace. Probably the greatest evangelist in the history of the church, besides the Apostle Paul, was George Whitefield. He believed in particular redemption and double-predestination, and it is said that he rarely preached a message without weeping for the lost.

Be careful about making careless statements that a belief in sovereign election and definite atonement kills one's zeal for evangelism and missions. These kinds of statements are based on ignorance.

HOW TO PRESENT THE GOSPEL ACCURATELY

1. All people are sinners, spiritually dead, and separated from God.
2. Because men are sinful, they are in rebellion against God.
3. God is holy and just, and must judge all rebellion against Him.
4. God will judge all men and women, and has promised eternal judgment for all who do not have their sins forgiven.
5. God is love, and sent His Son into the world to die for sinful people.
6. Christ died for the sin, curse, guilt, judgment, unbelief, and hell of all who believe in Him.
7. Christ died for sinners, and you are a sinner in need of a Savior, Jesus Christ.
8. You will know whether Christ died for your sins the moment you believe and trust in Christ.
9. You must change your mind (repent) about Christ and receive Him as your Savior from sin and the Lord (God) who has a right to rule in your life.
10. When you do believe, you will receive the forgiveness of sins and share Christ's life forever.
11. Whether you receive God's love or God's wrath is directly related to whether you believe that Christ died for your sins and that He is your Lord (God.)

CONCLUSION

I have been asked, "Doesn't it bother you, Dr. Arnold, to think about people in hell for whom Christ did not die?" My answer is, "Yes, it bothers me. But it bothers me a whole lot more to think about people in hell for whom Christ did die. To think that they are suffering eternal condemnation, when Christ died to keep them from it, horrifies me. This makes the death of Christ powerless to save." Dear readers, I would rather limit the extent of the atonement any day than limit the power of the atonement!"

Why is it so important to believe in Christ? Because He is the one who died for sinners. He substituted for sinners. He died in their place and stead. He bore their curse, unbelief, punishment, and hell. Any sinner who receives Christ through faith can declare with confidence, "Christ died for my sins!" Only Christ's death has the power to deliver from sin and to keep a man out of eternal punishment.

QUESTIONS:

1. From what you have learned from this chapter and from your study of the Bible, how would you define the issue raised in this chapter?

2. Explain the logic in the argument for limiting the substitutionary value of Christ's death to the elect only.

8. Write out some talking points for telling someone about limiting the extent of Christ's death vs. limiting its power. Include how this affects our view of God.

4. How does our understanding of the use of "all," "every," and "world" allow us to see Christ's atoning death as limited to the elect?